The Nighthawks Guide to Succeeding in College

Nighthawks Publishing

Nighthawks Publishing
The Nighthawks Guide to Succeeding in College

MLMC–Nighthawks
Northampton, MA

Published by MLMC–Nighthawks
29 Butler Place, #2
Northampton, MA 01060
http://www.mlmc-media.com

Nighthawks logo by Melissa Goldsmith.

ISBN: 978-1-63328-014-4

TABLE OF CONTENTS

Preface

The Nighthawks Guide to Succeeding in College is a handbook to help the new college student, whether traditional or non-traditional, do his/her best in the college or university environment. It includes a self-assessment test that helps students to better use the guide's advice, applying the writers' wisdom to their own unique situations and learning styles. Its chapters use a friendly, colloquial approach to address issues such as planning, time management, stress management, self-management, and relationships. Advice includes how to eat healthy, how to stay safe, how to avoid becoming overwhelmed, how to decide which classes to take (and avoid), when to take classes, and how to keep relationships with family and significant others from becoming a negative force. The guide constantly uses humor, wit , and memorable stories to make reading more fun—and to get points across clearly, leaving little room for misunderstanding. Above all, the guide is honest about the college experience; it does not try to sell students anything, nor does it use buzzwords just for the sake of seeming more relevant or cool. We make a genuine effort to neither talk over students' heads, nor talk down to them, while remaining friendly.

Success is a Decision You Make

How I Got Here

I don't remember how old I was when I decided I would go to college. It seems like I always just assumed I would. Reality has a way of catching up to people, though, and my parents couldn't afford to send me. Of course, I had the answer: I simply decided I would make good grades and earn scholarships. In my case, that plan worked.

But I know that I got lucky. I managed to win an academic scholarship to get my undergraduate degree, and when I decided that I was going to go to graduate school to make myself more marketable, I managed to get fellowships. So you could say that at least financially, I was set to get all the way through graduate school. The result was that I ended up with thirteen years of formal academic education. Like so many other graduates around the country, I know that I owe a huge debt of gratitude to the three institutions I attended to get the degrees I have today.

And like I said, financially I was set. But finding the money to go to college is just the first hurdle for the would-be graduate. Actually succeeding is the most important part of going to college. Being a successful college student means establishing the right priorities, making wise choices, becoming a master of time management, and most importantly, establishing beneficial relationships.

How My Story Can Help You

So now you know how I made it. But what can I offer you in the form of advice, you might be asking. After all, I was the kind of student who knew her whole life that she would attend college. Perhaps you find yourself surprised to be in college. Perhaps you were the kind of student who didn't think of education as an end in and of itself; you were just looking to graduate high school and join the workforce—but then found yourself changing your mind because of the job market or other forces beyond your control.

Maybe you were a struggling student, so you never even thought you could get into college, much less worry about succeeding there. Maybe it is your parents' wish that you attend college; as for yourself, you feel vaguely bewildered about an academic environment—even your major is what we call a "parental major," meaning you are getting your degree in something that mom and dad value; you yourself are ambivalent towards your chosen degree field. Maybe you are already working but need more education to achieve your professional goals—this means you'd be both working and putting yourself through college.

I may have always known I was going to get a college degree, but let me tell you, I did not have it easy. Coming from a poor family and being a first generation college student, I had no choice but to work to put myself through school. After all, scholarships paid for only so much. I am not saying I was ungrateful. I mean, they did help, but they did not cover all my costs.

No matter how you managed to get into the doors of your college, or why you're there, I hope to address your concerns. I have taught for ten years, and what I have gathered from fellow professors and from my students, as well as from my own experiences as a student, all have value. The bottom line is the advice I will offer in this guide worked for me, and it worked for them.

First Things First

Let me make a bold statement here—You must decide to succeed in college. Yes, it's that simple. Making that initial decision means that you will work to get your priorities in order.

As for me, I ended up getting a doctorate in English, but I laugh when I remember the first essay I wrote in college. I wrote it during class, and the topic was why I was there. I was eighteen and passionate, so I wrote that I didn't want a bunch of knowledge, just the tools to gain access to that knowledge. I figured I would likely never be approached on the street and asked who wrote "The Love Song of J. Alfred Prufrock" (unless the person who approached me was George from my Freshmen English class), but what I found out was that in everyday life, I encountered people and situations that required I had certain knowledge, and that I could build on that knowledge. This will happen to you, and how you choose to respond will affect your success in college, and in life.

Thinking back, I realize how naïve I was. But truth be told, I did accidentally hit on an important point: having the right tools makes all the difference. I want this guide to be just such a tool for you.

Before I begin offering you this advice, however, I will ask you to take a good look in the mirror. I want you to assess your skills and interests so you can design your own method of dealing with the vast amount of information you will receive in your college classes.

A Little Self-Knowledge Goes a Long Way

The following questionnaire will help you decide how to take the kind of notes during class that make sense and prove helpful when you refer to and study them later. It will also help you plan your classes. You can and should answer this questionnaire more than once during your time in college, especially if your interests change or you figure out that your plan isn't working, and you need to devote more time to studying, completing assignments, or getting help, in order to be more productive and successful. The questionnaire may also reveal something about your personality.

Having done all this, I can say that *your self-assessment is the primary tool needed to succeed in college*. None of us are cookie cutter people; everyone is a bit different, and we all learn, understand, and remember differently. Therefore, complete this questionnaire carefully. And most importantly, put what you learn from it to good use.

Final Note Before You Begin

And here is one final note: I will do my part to help. After you learn about your skills, interests, and personality, I will acquaint you with some further resources. Some of these services may be new to you, and here is where the voice of experience is valuable. Because of my experiences at different colleges and universities, both large and small, I can tell you they may be lifesavers; I cannot recommend them enough.

As a student, I discovered what services and people could help me get past writer's block, who to talk to in order to find more financial support and learn to efficiently save money on a student budget, and what to do when my roommate had oddly colored toenails (I discovered the difference between needing Student Health Services and the fashion police). If your situation is not addressed in this book, your college or university's Student Services Director or library will know how to help you find other resources.

But here is what you, as a student, must do: ask a lot of questions. You should never be afraid to ask questions, as you should never assume that your individual needs are first and foremost on the minds of people who are there to help not only you, but every student on the campus. If a service seems of potential interest to you, talk to the proper authority who can help—if you're a bit shy, pick up the phone, send an e-mail, or (in some cases) use available apps to make an appointment. These services are free of charge—you have already paid for them in your tuition, so make use of them!

The third section of this guide is devoted to time management and associated success strategies. These strategies are key—they will go a long way towards determining your success (or failure) in college. I know you've been inundated with the many books and even courses designed to teach some complicated method to slice your time into manageable pieces, so I will not add to that growing number. Rather than propose any one plan, this book will discuss several options from which you can choose.

I will also discuss something that is closely associated with time management, which is STRESS. Many colleges and universities hold stress management workshops, and I cannot recommend these enough. Consider them an essential part of your academic education. There are as many ways to relieve or cope with stress as there are stressed-out students, so again, I will not add to the number (and thereby add to your stress!). Instead, I will offer the voice of experience, having dealt with many of these stress reduction options myself. I can discuss these from two viewpoints: from my experience as a student and as a teacher—after all, I know which of these stress management techniques worked for my students.

This book will also discuss self-management, a hefty category that deals with elements such as personal responsibility, health, personal safety, and interpersonal relationships. Yes, I know you've been working on the latter for years now, but your life will change drastically once you enter college. More will be demanded of you on a daily basis, and you will need to develop relationships that allow you to meet those demands. If nothing else, this book may help you to develop lifelong personal relationships that foster your academic development, and believe me, very little is more important than this for students and professionals.

Okay, Time for You to Talk

Now I come to the end of my introductory comments. At this point, I need to ask you to join this discussion because, to put it bluntly, *no one knows you better than you*. I would like you to share your wisdom by doing the following personal assessment. As you read this guide, you can refer back to your answers to these 30 questions about yourself to see what best fits you (no, I will not ask what color you are, which Beatle you are, or what kind of cat you'd be—those kinds of self-assessment questions are best left to Social Media).

And after you're done, if you have advice that you would have included in this guide, please offer it by contacting MLMC Media-Nighthawks Publishing. Maybe I neglected an important category of college experience that you would like to see addressed in a future edition. I can't be everywhere or everyone, so I would be grateful for your contribution.

Now that you know what to expect from this guide, get ready to learn to succeed in college. As I said before, success is a decision—your decision. I can offer you the tools, but you must be willing to use them properly. After all, if you try to drive a screw with a hammer, you may succeed, but it would be difficult. No one needs to make life harder than it is—that just makes failure more possible. And if you approach any endeavor in life expecting to fail, you have a better chance of doing so.

It is not my intention to scare you with some of the examples I offer throughout this book. But the reality is that Freshmen are always at risk of failing in their first semester. If they aren't careful, they can end up suffering from eating disorders, family problems, poor interpersonal relationships, possibly even suicidal thoughts. It has always been my goal to not lose a single student to failure or anything else.

Personal Learning Assessment Tool

Skills and Interests

Knowing about yourself is the best way to know how you need to learn, *how learning fits into your larger goals in life*, and how you see yourself in the world as an educated professional. These 30 questions will get you started thinking about who you are, who you want to be, and what you want out of life. Your college experience is literally the first step towards becoming the person you want to be, doing what you want to be doing, living the life you want to live.

Questions

1. How do you process information? Do you examine it once quickly, or do you approach information in a methodical way, reading it closely then glancing at it later in review?

2. How do you learn best—by seeing new information, by hearing new information, or by both writing/drawing and hearing new information?

3. What is your favorite subject? Do you like it because it's easy to learn, or because it represents a challenge?

4. What is your least favorite subject, and why?

5. In your opinion, which basic skills do you need to improve?

6. Would you say you are a math person or a language person?

7. Are you more comfortable alone or in a group?

8. Would you rather stand out in a crowd or blend in?

9. What extracurricular activities do you enjoy?

10. Describe your work experience to date, then evaluate it. Did you enjoy it? Why or why not?

11. Do you have a career goal in mind? What made you choose it?

12. List the following, in order of importance to you, one being the most important:
- education
- family
- job
- fitness
- friends
- religion
- money
- self-expression/individuality

13. Are you shy or outgoing? Do you wish you were otherwise?

14. What are you afraid of? Try to think of three things.

15. Is there a role model you'd like to emulate, and why? This person does not need to be famous.

16. What qualities do you hate in a person, and why? Try to pinpoint the qualities you would strongly prefer to not have to incorporate into your own life.

17. Are you mechanically inclined? Do you prefer hands-on work or theoretical work?

18. When faced with a problem, do you have many ideas and have to sort them out, or do you have trouble generating options?

19. Do you have a learning disability?

20. How much noise or distraction can you tolerate? For instance, do you often find yourself in a room where the television and/or radio and personal computing devices are on simultaneously?

21. Would you rather spend most of your day indoors or outdoors?

22. If you could go anywhere in the world, including in the U. S. , where would you like to travel? What would you do when you got there?

23. If you could change one aspect of society, what would it be?

24. Do you enjoy taking risks, or would you prefer a safe, predictable environment?

25. Do you feel wide awake and happy in the morning, or are you most productive at night? You might try creating a chart that describes your energy level at various times during the day.

26. What are your hobbies?

27. What person has been the most positive influence on your life? What lessons did that person teach you?

28. What would you most like to change about yourself?

29. How do you react to criticism?

30. What is the most important thing in your life?

Chapter One: Planning Your Classes

Know Thyself, Then Schedule Your Classes

Now that you have written a short novel about yourself, it's time to put some of that self-knowledge to use. I cannot stress enough that before you tailor your classes to your interests, skills, and abilities, that you should work with your advisor (or team of advisors) to determine what is possible in your four college years, which can be neatly divided into two sections: your core courses and the courses in your major.

At most colleges, the better part of the first two years of college are made up of core courses, those courses that serve the purpose of making you a generally well-educated graduate. These usually include English (usually writing and sometimes literature), Math, Political Science and/or History, Psychology, and at some colleges, a Second Language and Physical Education (suffice it to say that very little has changed in the decades since I was a student). These core courses not only make you a well-rounded graduate; they may also help you find your path if you are uncertain about your major or if you have concerns about being able to graduate in four years. In short, colleges have over the centuries come to the wise decision that these are courses that should be required before students tackle the more difficult classes that deal specifically with their majors, whether those majors are art, biochemistry, business, engineering, history, literature, music, nursing, social work, or something else.

At this point, I would like you to review your answers to questions three through six. If your favorite subject is one of those that is identified as a General Education or core requirement, it would be a good idea to take a course related to it during your first semester. This will serve two purposes. It will help you maintain a high level of engagement or interest in college early on, and it will allow you to make a more informed decision about your chosen area.

The Dirty Work

Here's the bad news: you must face the fact that you will be required to take courses that you don't like, in areas or disciplines in which you may not even see any value. There is no magic bullet for this. The best suggestion anyone can make is that you should make the best of your situation by devoting just as much time and energy to these courses as you do to your favorites because they will affect your grade point average, and if you are applying for a job after graduation or applying to graduate school, your GPA is important.

In fact, because these required courses are often in areas which you have never pursued an interest, you may have to push yourself even harder, devoting even more time to them. This is normal and should be expected. I used to give myself a reward for studying the courses I didn't like—something small, but meaningful. In some cases, I would choose to just get these courses out of the way, saving my favorites for last. This helped me to sleep at night because I could drift off anticipating studying my favorite subject, which put into perspective the need to do "the dirty work" up front.

Honing Your Skills Early

The other important bit of information your self-assessment should tell you is whether you need to improve your study skills, based on your answer to question five. At most colleges and universities some type of Freshman year study skills course is required, and this can take many forms. No matter whether this course is called Study Skills, or The Freshman Year Experience, or First Year Seminar (or any other number of names depending on what is fashionable at the time), it will have as its goal the transitioning of your mindset, study skills, and expectations from high school to college.

This is to help you get over the fright you may feel during your first semester of college because you have no idea how to organize the large amounts of information being thrown at you; a course such as this introduces skills that you can use to become a better organizer of information and time. Some of these courses will also give you your first *cohort* experience, which is a fancy way of saying they encourage you to make friends and find people who have the same major, so you can begin the process of group-oriented learning. Some of these courses will even offer a *common experience*, usually in the form of a common reader; again, this is to encourage you to become communal in your study and learning habits—and to not fall into the trap of trying to survive without help from fellow students.

Two other basic skills that students often need help with early on are simple computation and writing, skills that you will be introduced to in core math and writing classes. College writing classes go by various names, such as Rhetoric, Composition, or sometimes simply English. Depending upon your ACT or SAT scores and your college or university, you may be required to take a developmental class in one or both of these subjects. Such courses typically offer you more contact time with instructors or tutors, a method of giving you one-on-one access to help when you are learning in an area that is unfamiliar to you.

When you take such courses, remember that even though instructor office hours and tutoring are optional, you should make using both a priority. It isn't often that people stop what they are doing to help you out of a tough situation, so use the offers from your professors and your institution's tutoring center wisely. The biggest mistake you can make as a student is not asking questions, and one-on-one tutoring sessions offer you just that opportunity—and a chance to get a detailed answer tailored to your individual learning style.

Finally, in classes such as these or any other, make sure you have access to the textbook. Remember that the textbook is there to offer you another way to learn the information, and more importantly, you can work at your own pace. If the class lecture moved too quickly for you, the textbook offers you the chance to control how long you should spend learning each concept. On more difficult or fundamental concepts (meaning the concepts upon which all other concepts in the course depend), you should (and can) spend more time. All of this advice is predicated on one important concept—that you have taken your education seriously.

Keep an Open Mind

I know that it is human nature to not take material seriously if you believe that it has no value in the "real world." For instance, my stepson was convinced he would never use skills he learned in geometry; he therefore resented having to take the course. As he became an adult, he discovered that he wanted to be a carpenter, and now he sincerely wishes he had devoted more time and attention to studying angles.

On the other hand, a friend of mine who was a carpenter studied public speaking after high school, and he is now an excellent communicator, using that skill to better market his trade. The point is that sometimes it is impossible to know what skills will be necessary in your future; in addition, your values and plans will change with time. Therefore, it is to your advantage to be flexible in your approach to scheduling classes that improve basic skills.

The secret to doing well in classes you wish you didn't have to take is to find some aspect of the subject area which you do like. You may discover, for instance, that your study group in a math class includes one of the most fascinating people you have met thus far in college, or you may discover in a literature class that the essays of Henry David Thoreau, who wrote a lot about nature and farming, resonate with you because of your childhood in a rural town.

If I sound optimistic here, it's because I am, and you'll need to be. I had very little to praise about my first biology course in college, but I found that the Biology Lab instructor helped me to understand concepts that had confused me during the lecture. By focusing my attention on the positive, I was able to learn, and later apply, some new basic skills.

Alt-Facts Will Get You Nowhere in College

Another skill that will vastly improve your success is research. Very few colleges or universities have a formal, for-credit information literacy or library research course, but *your ability to do your own research to supplement what you learn in class is absolutely essential.* You will also be preparing yourself to excel in your chosen future, because without new research, no field would ever grow, and we would never have advances in science, technology, psychology, social work, literary studies, or even music.

At many colleges, the Freshman year English courses are used as gateways into library research. It is likely that your writing instructor will require you to research your ideas that will make it into your assigned writing. This is fortunate, for when you take courses later in your major, you will be expected to know how to access *relevant* research material in the academic library.

That being said, if you are fortunate enough to be at a college or university that does offer a formal course in information literacy, I suggest taking it during your first year, so that you are not faced with the embarrassment of being a Junior or Senior who has to admit ignorance of research in your field to one of your professors. You don't want to be that student who has no idea how to begin a major research or capstone project or has never even been inside the library.

Learning to do research in your Freshman year will make you aware of many types of information resources, and more importantly, you will know how to gain access to them.

Get to Know Your Librarian

You will therefore want to be familiar with not only your library, but your librarian. In the age of computerized information, your librarian is the expert who can keep you from making mistakes like assuming a website is correct just because its creator says it is, or thinking that a fake news website (a website that knowingly and purposefully puts out false information for the sole purpose of misleading people) is giving you accurate stats and facts. Your librarian will also save you a lot of time, as he/she knows the most efficient way to search any type of database. You could spend hours looking for an article that your professor considers relevant to your research; your librarian will find it in less than 10 minutes, if not faster.

Working with your librarian is important *because college libraries are organized differently than public ones, and the databases to which academic libraries subscribe are more difficult to use than Internet search engines* (mainly because they offer so many more menu items that help make searches better). To use a metaphor, Internet search engines generally are bicycles—they have little functionality that allows you to find exactly what you want; databases are luxury automobiles, complete with dashboard functions that allow you to control every aspect of your driving. Your librarian will teach you to use this dashboard functionality.

Academic libraries differ greatly from both public libraries and the Internet in another important way: the academic library makes accessible not just popular articles from magazines, but also researched articles written by professionals in your field. These articles are more accurate because they are vetted by distinguished experts in that field. Such articles are published in what are called scholarly or peer reviewed journals, such as *The New England Journal of Medicine* or *The Journal of the American Medical Association*. Most Freshmen will enter college having not only never read these journals, but in many cases never even having heard of them.

Finally, the academic library is all about access. Librarians are hired for their ability to get college and university faculty and students anything they need for their research, even if it means borrowing it from other libraries. Depending on your college's policies, your librarian may be able to use a service called Interlibrary Loan to get you *anything* you need, *for free*, even if you are a Freshman. Your library very likely also belongs to a consortia, which is a group of libraries who agree to lend each other materials, and better yet, agree to let each others' students use their services.

The Student Success Center

Another resource you'll want to make use of is your campus's Academic Resource Center, and its affiliated Writing Lab. Writing labs are usually located in the library, in what is called a Student Success Center (or a similar name), or sometimes in the English Department. Most new college students have trouble transitioning to college-level writing, which is as different from high school-level writing as night is from day.

You will need to make use of the face-to-face writing tutors, software programs, apps, and online tutoring that are made available to you. After all, *writing is a skill which colleges and professional-level jobs both require*. Such tutoring centers exist to help students like you with the elements of writing that Freshmen find most troublesome: designing an argument, articulating a thesis, narrowing your focus, and knowing when you need to research a topic in order to write about it intellgently.

You've heard the old saying that you cannot get answers when you don't even realize there is a question. Well, college-level writing works that way. You can't know if you understand your topic if you haven't read about it or researched it. And if you don't understand your topic (especially if you don't know that you don't), then you cannot write about it intelligently.

Career Goals

At this point I would like you to review your answer to Question 11. If you have a career goal in mind, you might wish to take an introductory course to that field during your first year in college. It is important to remember that your first two years are the time when you should allow yourself the opportunity to decide if your major leads to the kind of job that you really want to do (remember, this will be for most if not all of your life). Without throwing yourself too far off-track as far as graduating in four years is concerned, you can experiment in this way. The beauty of this plan is it will prevent you from discovering too late that you have made a false start, which will make it impossible for you to graduate on time. You can usually take one or two courses in your field per semester, to test your skills and your interest level.

I began college with the misguided idea that I wanted to be a medical doctor, so I took an introductory biology course. I discovered, to my horror, that I did not like biology. More importantly, I discovered that I had trouble learning its basic concepts. So I fell back on the most important advice I had heard (which I discussed earlier in this book), which is to never shy away from asking questions. I talked with the instructor during his office hours and explained my situation. He gave me his perspective: he explained how hard the path would be that I was setting for myself. After some thought, I changed my major.

I do not for one minute want to suggest that your first encounter with a subject will determine the entire future of your career, or that your professor should control your decision-making process. The lesson I do want you to take away is that people who study and teach the field you are interested in know it inside and out, and can give good advice. They have the benefit of experience and can offer you another, more informed perspective about what challenges you are likely to encounter as a student and a professional.

Above all, remember that professors and instructors are there to help you succeed, not only in their classes, but as a student and as a person. Most of them will be happy to make an appointment to discuss your career interests—and your student frustrations. They are, after all, deeply enmeshed in a field you are just beginning to explore.

Once you've talked to them, ask yourself some questions, then take another look in the mirror. You might want to take another course in your major to see if your first impression was wrong, or you might simply shift focus and decide to take another path. One of my best friends started out as a chemistry major, and after two years discovered that he did not enjoy his courses, was not doing his assignments (for the first time in his life, as he was an A student), and was not making any friends because he did not like being around other chemistry majors. After some thought, he realized that on a fundamental level, he had little in common with them. He also met with his advisor and ended up switching majors. He lost only one semester, and more importantly, he was sure that he had made the right decision.

Learning Disabilities

Now I want you to look at your answer to question 19. Let's talk about learning disabilities. You may have gone all the way through high school without ever being tested, even though you have had trouble learning certain types of material. Perhaps you have had difficulty reading and have lost patience because words seem to jumble. Perhaps you look at numbers and draw a blank. Whatever the case, you should know that learning disabilities are complex, more of a spectrum than an answer to a YES/NO question. While you may not suffer from dyslexia or other learning challenges, you may still be somewhere on the disabilities spectrum.

At this point, the best advice I can give is be completely honest with yourself; you cannot get help if you don't even realize you need it. Ask yourself honestly about the hurdles you face when trying to learn, and do a little self-assessment. You want to do this for a very good reason: most colleges and universities have formal programs that exist solely to help students with disabilities. These programs are run by experts who know how to test students to determine whether they face serious disability-based challenges. These services are also very private, since these experts know that students who get diagnosed with disabilities often either wish to remain anonymous or become self-conscious; if you are one of these students, you probably don't want to be known just for your disability. The bottom line is that you should not be hesitant to seek assistance for fear that labels will stigmatize you. Colleges and universities that offer services for disabled students know how to keep your private business private.

Your instructors are not trained to recognize whether you have a learning disability. Only an expert will be able to determine if there is a problem—but only if you consult him/her. Once you can honestly deal with the reality of a learning challenge, you and your college's disability expert can work with your instructors to identify the resources available that can make your college experience more successful. Some of the most brilliant people I know, professors included, are dyslexic, or possess other learning disabilities. They succeeded despite this.

Two Case Studies

Let me share with you a truly amazing experience: I had a student who sat in the back row, always gazing at the wall to his left. When I collected homework, I never received anything from him. After two weeks of this, I asked him to come to my office; I urged him to pay more attention in class. He behaved strangely, peering closely at the poster on my wall, and when he left I was unsure if he had understood my plea that he apply himself. The next week, he again turned in no homework. Finally, I had to ask him to my office again to explain that he needed to drop the course if he didn't want to fail. Soon after, his mother called me: she had not known that her son was not turning in homework or understanding concepts discussed in class. She told me that he had a learning disability but did not wish to be stigmatized in college. As it turns out, during high school he was ostracized because of his disability.

Had I known this information from the beginning (I still don't know what his disability was), I could have pointed him to the Access Office at my college, which helped students like him. I would have met with him more often to address his concerns. What he did not understand was that from my side of the desk, he seemed to be lazy and uninterested in class; sometimes I wondered if he was coming to class while high. I know this sounds like a harsh judgment, but instructors and professors are people too, and when we have limited information, we cannot make accurate judgements about students and therefore cannot help them as much as we might like. In his case, I was sadly wrong.

Contrast this to the case of another one of my students. She came to college expecting to succeed, as she had earned excellent grades during high school. She was the kind of student who worked twice as hard as others to insure her success. She put in long hours on her studies and therefore had no time for a social life, so she went to the Access Office to get tested. She had dyslexia. The Access Office taught her new study skills and techniques that allowed her to absorb information more quickly. She began to have time for a social life, and she began to enjoy her study time, instead of dreading it.

Learning Styles

We are all individuals. We all process information in our own unique way. Take a look back at your response to question one—your answer will give you an idea about your own methods. If you tend to process information once, in a slow and methodical way, then review it later, then you need to plan to apply this method to your courses. If you read your sociology assignment Thursday in preparation for a Friday exam, you will want to review it quickly before class, so you know you'll need a little pre-exam preparation time. If, however, you skim first, then examine information more carefully, you should plan to leave more time, for a thorough review.

If you are a slow, methodical person like me, you can schedule your classes on Monday, Wednesday, and Friday, making Tuesday and Thursday your review days—and you can alternate reviewing with other tasks and interests. If you are the speedy type, you will want to provide time gaps in your schedule so that you can give your complete attention to the review the second you begin it.

I have a good friend whose memory is contextual—in other words, he remembers information when his memory is jogged by a sound or a sight. He also learns by looking at how ideas are connected. So he would briefly review his notes the night before each exam by thinking of them in terms of a narrative, with each idea causing or influencing the next. But more importantly, he would show up as early as possible to the exam room to re-read his notes in the desk where he would take the exam; he knew that items in the room would jog his memory when it came to recalling details. He studied for all his history exams this way.

Know Thy Methods

Knowing how you learn will help you to space out your class schedule, with courses taken either back-to-back or with gaps in between. But what time should you schedule which classes? Take a glance at the chart you prepared in response to question 25. You should schedule your classes during your peak times, the times when you are most alert. No one wants to be a sleepy student, especially since sleepy students are often confused with apathetic students. Why risk making your instructor think you simply don't care about physics, when in fact you like science but just can't stay awake at 8:00 a.m.? Energy tends to come in stretches, so take advantage of those blocks of time when you feel most energetic—those stretches are the best times to take your classes. You should still have some peak energy times left, so this is when you should study or do out of class assignments.

Keep in mind that we don't live in an ideal world. I once worked an overnight shift and then had to force myself to stay awake to take advantage of my 8:00 am until noon peak time to study and take classes—before napping during the afternoon. I didn't like missing out on an entire day, but I had no choice. Also realize that sometimes you will not be able to tailor your schedule to your personal peak times. The best you can hope for is to match some of your body clock with your class schedule.

Identify Your Weaknesses

So now you have allowed for both your information-processing method and your personal peak times in planning your classes. You have taken your interests into account, without forgetting you need to take some general, core, and basic skills courses. You have taken learning disabilities into account and learned how to address them so you can have both a college career and a social life. You have looked at your favorite and least favorite courses.

From this point, you should begin choosing classes with another consideration in mind: your personality. Review your answers to questions 13 through 16. If you said you were shy, I have news: you would be well served to take some kind of oral communication course, perhaps even a speech course. If you wish you weren't shy, you'll probably be happy to jump in with both feet. If you are terrified at the thought of public speaking, you will have to give yourself some time to adjust to college before you undertake this necessary task, so you may want to wait. If, on the other hand, you are outgoing, you might actually enjoy not only a course that involves communication, but even a career that does—and obviously, you'll have no excuse to not jump right in.

Consider question 14. If you are afraid of science classes in general, be realistic when you plan your schedule. Do not take sociology, psychology, biology, and chemistry during the same semester, even if you are under the impression that you could get these courses out of the way. You have to be careful to not make yourself miserable. You may end up becoming one of those ghost students who shows up on a class roster but never comes to class, or shows up only on occasion.

Even though you know you cannot succeed this way, you'll end up making yourself so scared or depressed that you'll sabotage your own success. You should schedule courses so that you are likely to enjoy at least one of your classes per semester. In other words, strive for balance in your schedule. It's perfectly fine to deal with one or two courses you're afraid of per semester, but don't overdo it. You'll become overstressed or even physically ill.

Don't Be a Hater

Now look at your answer to number 16. This is a really tough question, and I have a complicated reason for asking it. Many of us arrive at college with prejudices. To pre-judge someone is to jump to a conclusion about him or her without sufficient information. Could you answer the second part of the question? If you can't be specific about what you despise, you might just have a prejudice or lack of sufficient information. You may believe yourself to be different and possibly even better than some types of people. Ask yourself why.

I am not attempting to change your opinion here; I'm simply asking you to think deeply. You should always challenge your own prejudices and ask yourself why you hate subject areas or types of people. This is important in academia because universities and colleges are awash with diversity, both in people and ideas; it's one of their main reasons for their existence. If you are going to survive in the world, you will have to learn to listen, and the college environment is no different. Interrupting the political activists or that preacher in the quad is not going to be productive—it probably won't even silence either.

Colleges and universities practice academic freedom, which is the right to free speech in and beyond the classroom for the purposes of teaching and learning. Diversity is something you can learn to embrace, no matter where you come from. That student with the purple hair, black toenails, eyebrow piercings, oversized jewelry, and differing opinions may just be the nicest person you will meet in class. Sometimes differences of opinion are just about lifestyle choices. I had a college roommate who spent more money on an outfit than I made in a month. I had to learn to accept that her lifestyle was something I would never understand, but that we could still have a friendly relationship.

Know What You Want

Do not expect to finish four years of college without encountering people or ideas that shock you, shake you to the core of your being, and cause you to question your assumptions about life. This may seem a frightening experience, but you should welcome it. It is part of growth. And more importantly, the academic campus is a safe place to grow.

In college, you can ask yourself questions about who you are at your core and who you'd like to become, which includes what you would like to do throughout your life. And guess what. The other students around you are likely doing the same thing. Even though our identities are tied to our families, friends, hobbies, and passions, each of us is a unique individual, and that is a good thing for us personally and for society.

Review your answer to question 23. What did you say you would like to change about society? This might give you a good answer to what your college goal should be, and by extension, which courses you should take. I had the pleasure of course eavesdropping (I do this a lot; it can be a great way to learn) on a social work course my last semester before I retired. I became interested and began to stand outside the classroom to catch the lecture.

In fact, this may be one of the unconscious reasons I'm sitting here, writing this guide. It made me think about my attitude as a teacher toward younger people, and look back at my own college experience. Look at your answer to question 23 as a clue to a career path, or at least an interest you might not have realized before. I suppose I have always wanted to teach, at least since I was in second grade and our class read to the kindergarteners. I helped the kid who sat behind me in class in high school. Maybe you too can uncover a secret interest.

Next, look at your answer to question 26. Students tend to neglect their hobbies during college. They feel they do not have the time to pursue them anymore, and maybe you don't (we'll address time management later).

Suppose you like to swim. Here's what you can do about it. You can practice your hobby, meet your course obligations, and and relieve stress, all at the same time. Your hobbies are activities that you enjoy, so try not to abandon them without good reason. You will feel better and approach your other courses with more energy and a better attitude if you can find a way to incorporate your hobbies into your plans. Understanding your need to pursue hobbies, along with looking at your answer to question 27, will make your life better.

Question 27 can tell you quite a bit about your personality. The qualities you find valuable in your most positive influence are probably qualities you wish you possessed. My father was good at math because he was an electrician; I didn't even like math, but when he gave me complicated physics problems to solve, I would enjoy doing them because of my admiration for him. I became better at math and reasoning. Perhaps the person you admire didn't teach you in such a direct way; however, you did learn from this person, and college is your chance to develop the qualities you admire—plan your classes so that you can become that person. Just because you aren't good at something doesn't mean you cannot learn to be. That, again, is one of the reasons you are in college. Take an art class even if you are baffled by your grandmother's paintings but you love them. Following in the footsteps of someone you admire is a great motivator.

Now go back to question 15. You may be starting to see a pattern emerge. If your role model is a famous person, you can emulate that person after learning about him or her—and you can plan your courses accordingly. Aunt Jill may be your role model (even if she didn't go to college to get where she is), and if she is, ask her advice. Ask her how she achieved her goals. You can plan your classes so that you can emulate her. If she is self-educated, she can still tell you what she wished she could have learned in college.

The Next Steps

Now that you have used the information from your questionnaire to plan your first classes, you should begin to decide how you will manage the following areas of your life: your time, your stress, and your relationships. The following chapters will address these areas of your life and offer you strategies. These areas are rather artificially divided, as these categories overlap. But all of these areas can and should be managed so that you do not become overwhelmed or place yourself in danger. We all follow certain paths, so choose yours wisely.

Chapter Two: Time Management

Time to Take Stock

You may be the proud owner of a beautiful time-management device. It could be a state of the art personal device, either a cloud-based calendar that sends you reminders or an app that you've downloaded, or if you're old school, it could be a handsome journal-type calendar book full of pages that track every day, showing blocks of space to account for every hour.

Regardless of whether you manage your time via device, laptop, book, or even a series of post-it notes (physical or virtual), if you don't have time management skills, your planner is nothing more than a toy. In college, my own personal planner (a rather chic looking calendar book) became my very own fashion accessory. I carried it with me the first two weeks of college. After all, it looked cool and matched my personality perfectly. However, after a few weeks, I buried it beneath the textbooks in my room—where it could do me little to no good. Back then, I considered myself a creative person, an artist in the making and a rebel at heart, so I balked at the notion that my days should be so conveniently and efficiently planned.

Looking back, I have to admit that the passage of time has taught me about the necessity of time management. What I can tell you from where I sit now is that you, as a new college or university student, must use some method of time management. Only you and you alone can do this for yourself because truth be told, as you become a college student, you will find that suddenly, and without warning, you will very likely be on your own. While living with your parents and going to high school, you lived in a world where simply knowing how to set an alarm clock was enough. That is about to change as you enter dormitory or apartment life. You will need some method—or methods—of dividing up your now precious time so that you can get *every* assignment for *every* class done in time to meet *every* deadline, without losing *every* bit of sanity you possess.

Planning and Planners

This may seem very old school, but one of the best ways to account for your time is to build or make your own planner. There is no such thing as one size fits all planning, and as a corollary, there is no one size fits all planner, so creating your own allows you to personalize your planning to your individual needs.

At this point, review your answer to question two. If you are the kind of person who is visually oriented, you'll want to create some kind of visual planning device. You can either flex your artistic skills and draw up a table

(I suggest a calendar-based, seven-day table) in your planning book, or you can use a spreadsheet or word processing program to create a computerized table. Again, what is important is that you are the one creating the table.

Obviously, you'll want to label the columns after the days of the week, but don't forget the weekend. You may not have classes then, but you will want to use some Saturday and Sunday blocks of time for study and assignments. My second piece of advice to you is to schedule your classes and study times according to your peak energy times. You should do this on a weekly basis.

The Study Group

Most college programs encourage group work, even on assignments. This is because employers are becoming more and more aware that a person's ability to work as part of a team is extremely important, if not essential. Fortunately for you, studying as part of a group is an excellent time management skill. As soon as you know what your assignments are, you should form a study group that meets regularly, especially if you answered in the self-assessment that you would rather be in a group and blend in with the crowd.

The beauty of the study group is that you won't be responsible for every detail. Your study group will consist of different personality types with different skill levels, so you will be able to benefit from others who understand certain concepts better than you—and can possibly explain them so that you finally do understand. By the same token, you can contribute in those areas that are your strengths, possibly even teaching your fellow students. There is no better way to learn a concept than to explain it to someone else, so you will be honing your own skills as you go.

You may not need a study group for all of your classes, but try this option for at least one if you think it will suit your personality; if it turns out to be beneficial, you can try it for various classes.

Notes and Lists

I am a compulsive note taker and list maker, so I subscribe to what I call The Note and List Method. I recommend it highly if you consider yourself a creative person. I keep a list of things to do each day with me at all times. When I was a student I used to keep a very detailed list, including my class times and rooms. Even though I could have easily remembered some of this information, I felt satisfied when I could check items off of my list.

If you prefer keyboarding over writing by hand, you can create born digital lists, which you may or may not choose to print. You can come up with various methods of categorizing and storing your lists on your laptop or device. At times I have had as many as a dozen different folders, each with at least two levels of sub-folders, in which I kept my lists and notes.

Although it is difficult to use a computer or device for it, a variant of the Note and List would be the Sticky Note Method. Here the advantage is that you can move items around at will, which allows for great flexibility and last minute changes without messing up a table or list. One of my friends back in college used to place these notes on his dorm room walls, on his door, on his desk—basically every available surface. He literally ran his college life using little notes. Another student who was taking a poetry course used her own version: she would write one or two lines of a poem on each note, and then use her walls as an area to cut and paste these lines into complete poems. Every time she had an idea for a line or two, she would create a note. Still another friend would place notes containing inspirational quotes all over various surfaces, including the dashboard of his car—these weren't so much to remind him to do things as to remind him that he could handle anything college life threw at him. They served an important purpose in that they picked up his spirit whenever he felt down or overwhelmed. Still another friend uses the Post-It Note program on her computer. Even after she graduated and went into the workforce, she continued to use this program.

I will admit that people who overuse the sticky note approach vex me a bit (and sometimes scare me), but what I have learned over time is that we all have unique time management styles. These people did what worked for them, even if their methods might seem extreme to the average table creator or Note and List person.

Another version of Note and List is what I call The Notebook Method, or what could be more properly called The Notebooks Method, since it normally involves making a separate notebook for each class, listing class meeting times and rooms on the front. You can put all class material and notes in this notebook. You may even want to type these notes up once you get done with your classes for the day, or over the weekend. A friend of mine who had a troubled high school experience and went to college later in life re-typed all her notes and placed them neatly into a binder, from which she would study. Her organization skills made up for her lack of college preparation, and she ended up on the Dean's List and as a valued member of her university's Student Government Association. I have never been more proud of anyone in my life as I was of her when I witnessed her receiving her awards at graduation.

Phone a Friend

The Friend Method is a bit unorthodox, but it is a tried and true method of time management. Let me begin by warning you that if you use this method, you had better make sure that your friend is faithful and dependable. What I and many college students have discovered is that sometimes you can find a roommate or friend who is willing to schedule classes at the same time as you. You can then help each other by reminding one another when assignments are due; this person can even become your study partner or a member of your study group. Here I must offer a word of caution—don't try this with a roommate you hardly know.

The Deadline Method

The Deadline Method would not be my first choice, but it does work for people who thrive in high stress situations. Basically, it is the practice of prioritizing tasks so that every deadline is met, which of course means de-prioritizing other tasks. For example, during midterms you may decide to concentrate on which exam is next, at the expense of other exams or assignments, reasoning that you can easily switch gears and meet the next deadline, then the next, and so on.

This can work for highly organized people who can be task-oriented and are not prone to the lures of multi-tasking. It works well if you are the kind of person who can lose yourself in a large task for hours on end. It doesn't hurt if you're a table or list maker, by the way, since what you're doing in effect is checking off one task after another, trusting that you have calculated the time needed on each task correctly. When it does work, it allows you to devote appropriate study and work time to each exam and assignment.

It also works if you want to prioritize not based on deadlines but on skills and comfort level. Perhaps a math assignment is easier for you than an English paper that is due at about the same time. If this is so, you can prioritize based on whether you prefer to finish difficult tasks first, or save them until last. In the above example, you may reason that the English paper should be your priority because it takes more effort and energy for you to do well, and you may hedge your bet that you can do the math assignment (or prepare for a math exam) in less time—and do better because you won't have the paper nagging at the back of your mind.

Get a Calendar

You can't overestimate the effect that keeping a calendar can have on your time management. The good news is that there are as many types of calendars as there are students. Those who use gmail are already aware that it comes with a built-in calendar that allows users to not only track their tasks but to also receive reminders in the form of pop up notes or emails. Most personal devices will offer apps which perform a similar function, acting as both calendar and alarm clock.

If you're print oriented, you can easily find an oversized calendar that leaves plenty of room for note taking. You can also easily find whiteboard calendars that use dry erase markers. Businesses use these all the time because they allow for information to be seen with a quick glance, without having to boot up a computer or device (I can't tell you how many times I have shut down my computer only to realize I forgot to check my calendar, so I had to boot it up again—and wait). You can place one on your door so that the last thing you always see before leaving is your tasks for the day.

After the first week of classes, you will have a nice collection of syllabi and assignment sheets, either in print or virtually, through whatever course management software your college or university uses. Your calendar can become your course plans, where you can track all of your responsibilities in one spot. This would allow you to track due dates of all assignments and dates of all exams. Knowing the full range of tasks you need to complete for the semester allows you to carefully plan your time.

For example, if once you create your calendar you notice that you have two exams and two papers due on the same week, you can decide that it might be in your best interest to write one of those papers early (you can even mark on your calendar your artificial due date—the due date which you are giving yourself on the early paper). In addition, as you receive daily homework, you can add it to your calendar.

The Syllabi Method

All of your instructors and professors will give you a syllabus for their class. You should make sure these are accessible, in print or electronically, everywhere you go, especially if you go to the library or student study area of your college or university. Some syllabi are more detailed than others, and it is possible that you will be given a syllabus that lists every assignment for the course. If you are a list type of person, you can print or make a copy of your syllabi and use it as an assignment list. All you need do is cross out or mark each assignment as you complete it; in addition, you can highlight parts of the syllabus to mark information that you need to review before an exam.

More on Time Management

Let's take a detailed look at time management. You can choose pretty much any method, but whatever you choose as a method, you must stick with it. ***You must make it a priority to consult your calendar, list, table, or syllabus at least once a day.*** You have to use your method to figure out your best possible study time—not only what time of day that you choose, but how much time you can and should devote to studying.

You should keep in mind this time-tested rule, sometimes called the 1:3 rule. This ratio means that for every credit hour a course is worth (most courses are three credit hours), you should devote three hours of studying and/or finishing out-of-class assignments. Let's apply this rule to a scenario: You have enrolled in English Composition (which may at your college be called Rhetoric or Introduction to Writing), a three-credit hour course. Somewhere in your weekly schedule you will have to find nine hours to study for and/or complete assignments (likely papers) for that course.

I have more advice involving the number three. Always go over material three times. If you are the methodical type who reads things only once (and hopefully slowly), I suggest you change your tactic. It is better to first read information carefully, then skim it in review, then read it again while taking notes of the specific bits of information you find most challenging. Doing this, you have performed three operations on that text, and it should stay in your memory.

Remember when question two asked how you best learn? Well, if you are a visual person, someone who loves pie charts and drawings, your note taking can take the form of a graphic representation of the material. If you are a list maker, the notes can be a list. If you're highly organized, the notes can be an outline. The possibilities are endless because you can cater exactly to your own needs. Reading and writing or diagramming reinforce learning. And if you perform at least three operations on a text, you are more likely to recall the information. If you're a word oriented person, you will end up reading the information twice, then summarizing it once.

The Rule of Three

This rule of three will improve your understanding of class material. Let's look at some more real-life examples: Let's say that Celeste has a block of study time on Wednesday, from three to six. She needs to study English, math, and psychology, each a three credit hours course (meaning she will need 27 hours total). According to our rule of three, she should realize that she will need to study also on Monday and Friday—to complete the 27 hours of study time. She develops a plan.

She knows that she will need to take a short break every hour to get up and stretch, get something to drink, or eat a snack so that she can learn without the distractions of hunger, thirst, fatigue, and/or boredom. But the questions is how she will study. Since Celeste is a skimmer, she reads things once, and quickly. She decides to study English from 3:00 to 4:00. She skims her notes or text, reading it once carefully while looking up words she isn't understanding, then summarizes the information. She has satisfied the rule of three for her English assignment. Now she can have her break.

From 4:15 until 5:00 she plans to study math, specifically solving word problems. She skims each problem and highlights key words, then works on finding solutions. Since each problem emphasizes a theorem or equation she will need to understand, she writes her process in a notebook, possibly even repeating each one aloud. By this time, she has skimmed, highlighted, solved, and repeated, so she has performed four operations during the 45 minutes devoted to math.

Psychology is Celeste's favorite subject, so she saves it for last as a kind of reward for finishing her English and math studying. After Celeste is done with math, she takes a break, and at 5:15 she begins to study psychology, which introduces a number of new terms. As she skims the assignment, she underlines unfamiliar words, then looks them up in the glossary or a dictionary (a physical book or online dictionary). She reads the assignment once, and carefully. She has been asked to write three brief analyses, so she does so. Celeste has now satisfied the rule of three for all three subjects, but for only one hour each. She will need to repeat these processes *for each course*.

First and Last

Yet another rule will help you stay on track, and that is that people tend to remember the first and the last thing they are told. Celeste had satisfied her rule of three, but could not recall a particular math equation. So, she took time to look at math again before dinner. This gave her a better chance of recalling the information.

Let's apply this memory trick to the classroom. In some cases, your instructor can help—I used to begin my classes by asking students to write a paragraph about what they read in preparation. That caused them to anticipate and begin thinking about class discussion. As the discussion proceeded, students would ask questions, and I would offer answers or ask questions in return, as a way of gauging how well they understood the assignment. At the end of class, I would give them an out-of-class assignment.

I had a reason for conducting my class this way: I was aware that it is always easiest to remember first and last information, so I made them express their own thoughts first, then reinforced their knowledge during discussion, then reminded them about the next assignment, a way of giving them a preview of what would be discussed at the next class meeting and getting them to start thinking again.

As a student, you can find ways to apply the rule of the first and last for yourself. In fact, you probably use it already. Don't you normally make a last-minute effort to study for exams, sometimes while you wait in your seat? This is because you hope you remember that most recent information you reviewed.

Cramming May Work, but Plan for the Long Term

In time management, long-range planning is essential. In fact, if you are the kind of person who tends to procrastinate until the last minute, you should pay particular attention to long-term planning. You are playing a cruel joke on yourself if you attempt to study for a final exam by reviewing information that you are seeing for the first time. You are fooling yourself if you think you can do well in your classes by forcing yourself to stay awake all night, swilling coffee, attempting to create a well-planned essay that was assigned three weeks before. Not only will the lack of craftsmanship show in your essay, but you will also wander into the classroom looking and feeling like a zombie.

I believe people put things off not because of a lack of skills or interest, but out of fear. To the procrastinator, the assignment looked overwhelming, so he or she put it away, only to have to worry about it later. The problem with this tactic is that "later" turns into the day before something is due. No one can excel under such circumstances; it's not fair to you to place yourself under that much pressure.

If you're that procrastinator, here's what you should have done: First, break the assignment down into manageable pieces as soon as possible after you receive it. Determine what you're being asked to do by highlighting key words; consulting resources such as further reading, tutors, or classmates; and organizing your ideas, perhaps by outlining, concept mapping, making notes, or writing a summarized version of your paper. Since you started right away, you have time, which means that will have plenty of opportunity to develop ideas and refine thoughts later. You don't have to labor under the assumption that the first sentence you write should be worthy of a Pulitzer Prize—in fact, you should plan to at some point throw it out in favor of a better sentence. Therefore, don't be too quick to judge your first effort. Think of your work as if it were a human being. When you start, it's in its infancy. Given time and care, it will grow into a refined person with its own unique strengths. You should remember this for any involved work—give yourself time to approach each and every project step by manageable step.

Above all, never be shy of admitting when a task is over your head or beyond your skill set. You remember those resources you identified? Well, in the case of a writing assignment, one of your resources will be the Writing Lab. If you don't have time or cannot get an appointment, try using a classmate or even a roommate as a sounding board; sometimes all you need is a new perspective. This person doesn't even have to be in an English course to be helpful. She can simply help by letting you know if your sentences make sense and if your approach to the assignment is a logical one.

The Importance of Written Skills

Since I broached the subject of writing, I guess now is as a good a time as any to break the bad news to you. In many forms, and in many of your courses, you will be asked to write while in college. Like most people, you may have unreasonable fears of writing, one of which is the idea that you are supposed to produce a masterpiece every time (the fear I mentioned previously). ***Here is the reason I think so many students fear writing—they see writing as a talent—talents are gifts, skills given to us at birth—you either have the gift or you don't.*** Believe me I understand. I grew up believing that I wasn't given the writing gift. I used to say, "please ask me to operate a table saw; I can do THAT!" What you have to understand is that when you think this way, you give in to fear. The truth is that writing can be an art, and it can be a craft, but like playing a musical instrument or shooting a basketball, ***it is a skill that can be learned***, if given time and sincere effort. People don't ask the beginning carpenter to make a staircase; they ask him to saw the boards. In other words, you learn writing though methodical steps. This is what I did, and having done this, I want to offer you several methods that have proven useful for me. These are methods I then passed on to my students.

The first step in the writing process should generate ideas. How you do this is completely up to you. The options are endless, but include making a list, brainstorming into a recording device, concept mapping (drawing a diagram consisting of circles containing key words and then connecting those circles based on similarities), interviewing an expert, checking a book out from the college library, and/or finding and downloading a relevant article containing preliminary material on your subject. This process should allow you to not only gather, but also sort some ideas.

As soon as you have generated ideas, make a start at actually writing, even if you just finish one paragraph. As an alternative, you can outline the entire writing project, with a few details and examples. Whatever you do, don't trap yourself by thinking you have to write the introduction or the first paragraph first. If you do that and you get stuck, you won't get anywhere.

If you find yourself suffering with writer's block, this would be a good time to consult with a tutor or fellow student, or perhaps make an appointment with your professor. Sometimes you have a good idea what you want to write, but just don't know how to get that first sentence down—in such a case a sounding board can help. Whatever the case, do not allow yourself to procrastinate. This stage is the planning stage, the one where you prioritize ideas and begin to shape them into manageable sections, so you have to let the ideas flow. If you need a break, walk away for a bit and let the ideas you have already collected simmer a bit, then come back and repeat the process.

What you will have done is completed the process of idea generation (and possibly first draft writing) by completing its component parts. Rather than trying to make that staircase all at once, you worked on each board, each railing, and the bannister, and put them together in some logical order. But now remember that writing is a craft, so now you need to refine your product. This is where you need to make sure you know the requirements of style, mechanics, grammar, and whatever else your professor requires (such as research requirements).

Hints for Note Taking

Note taking is another academic skill, and like writing, it can be made more effective through practice. As a first-year college student, you may not have the slightest idea of how to take notes well, and that is understandable. Not all high schools are equal in how well they prepare students for college classes, and even if you were an A student in high school, you may still be at a loss to take meaningful and practical notes both in your college classes and on your courses' out-of-class review material. I hope here to offer you some tips that will help you hone this skill. Even if you feel confident about your ability, you may learn something to make your note taking even better.

First and foremost, unless you can write shorthand, accept that you will never be able to write as quickly as your professors can speak. One way around this problem is to ask your professors early in the semester if it's permissible to record lectures. If so, you're in luck. You can attend class, record lectures, and listen at a time when you can take careful notes. In fact, this method works well for those of you who prefer to listen and soak up information (rather than try to listen and take notes simultaneously), then review it later. For those of who don't like listening to taped lectures, note taking is the only alternative. The skill you then would have to hone is learning to identify key issues in real time. Your professor or instructor is not going to continually say "this is information on which you'll be tested," so you have to assume that any information given in lecture is important. Whether or not the instructor writes lecture notes on a chalkboard, whiteboard, or smartboard, shows you a diagram of it, or provides a handout, you as a student are responsible for learning key issues, theories, and terms. The good news is that these are likely to be repeated or discussed in some detail during class. If you hear something for the third time, assume it is a key issue—and assume you will be required to understand it in some detail.

I reiterate here that shyness is the biggest enemy for college students. If need be, ask your instructor to repeat something you missed. Remember, your professors and instructors want you to succeed, but you are responsible for your own learning. If I am your professor, and I whizzed past something important in my lecture, did not get questions from you about it in discussion, and did not get questions from you about it after class, I assume that you understood it. That means that ultimately, I will hold you responsible for any questions based on this information that show up on exams. If there is a one-two knockout punch for student learning, it is this: ask questions and take careful notes.

Those of you who are visual learners can make drawings of nearly any information. For example, you can draw a pie chart expressing the populations of China, America, and Africa as percentages, or you can diagram biological information in an outline of a human body. More importantly, you can do these things during a class lecture, possibly even using multi-colored ink to separate information into categories that you have created. The bottom line is that note taking is an essential skill; done well, it will help you learn despite the massive amounts of information you will be exposed to as a college student.

I suggest that you take time before you begin each class to consider what method you will use. Once you have decided, don't treat every class lecture as if it exists in a vacuum. It would benefit you to always review the previous lecture's notes in preparation for an upcoming class, since the information is continuous. This is a great strategy that will help you avoid the dreaded feeling of arriving at midterm week having forgotten everything except what was covered in the most recent lecture.

Other Possibilities

Learn and practice mnemonic devices, or memory strategies. As an ex-teacher of writing classes, I will give you an acronym-based one here. In fact, I remember using it myself for knowing when I had constructed a solid paragraph. The acronym is RENNS. To write a good paragraph, always remember to include Reasons, Examples, Names, Numbers, and Statistics.

The beauty of acronyms is that they are easy to create, so you can create your very own to help you learn related concepts—just take the first letter of each term and make an acronym. As long as you are clear about the definition of each term, you'll do well on any exam question that asks you to explain how they concepts relate.

Some people find it easier to recall information if they make it into a song or rap, since rhymes make a line easier to remember. To remember lists of items, some find it effective to create a visual image including all the items in that list. If you have a sense of humor, you could even turn information you need to remember into riddles or jokes. The point is, when it comes to mnemonic devices, there is not one-size-fits-all device. You have to discover the one that works for you.

Learning Styles

By now you have figured out that there are many ways to learn information, each unique to individual students. These are commonly called learning styles, and the idea of learning styles includes various elements, which we won't get into here. But what I will do is share some information that I myself had to learn in education classes.

The first is a very basic concept: There are at least four levels to learning: recognition, recall, analysis, and synthesis. Your goal is to master all four so that you master synthesis, which is the ability to understand a concept so well that you can apply it to a situation with which you have never been presented before (if you think about it, this is the skill you use daily, especially on a job, since you can never anticipate every event or problem that could occur on a given day).

But let me digress a bit. Before you can do anything else with new information, you need to be able to recognize it. You have to recognize that *metaphor* is a literary term and that it has something to do with language. If you reach the recall stage, it will be easy for you to match a term to its definition on a matching test. For example, you may be asked to show you know a literary term like *metaphor* by matching it to its definition, which is a comparison which does not use the words "like" or "as" but simply states that one thing is something else, like saying a pizza you ordered at the end of a long day is "just what the doctor ordered."

The third level, analysis, requires a learner to deconstruct and then reconstruct a concept, to take it apart and explain the function of each of its elements as part of the whole. If your writing instructor were to ask you to deconstruct the basic essay into its five parts, for the purpose of getting you to understand and explain the function of each of those five parts, you would be analyzing the concept of the essay.

The fourth level, synthesis, requires that you group concepts or ideas for the purpose of learning to differentiate between seemingly similar concepts. You would use analysis and synthesis to differentiate between a *metaphor* and a *simile*, which does use the words "like" or "as," as when you say, for example, that you aced an exam "like a boss." If your history professor were to ask you to compare the Korean, Vietnam, and Iraq wars, you would be both comparing these events for their similarities (what do wars have in common and what similarities did these particular conflicts share) and their differences. The purpose of this analysis and synthesis is to give you a deeper understanding of history and politics by teaching you to see even tiny differences.

Obviously, recognition is the most basic of these learning levels; recall is more difficult. Analysis requires not only more information but also critical thinking, and synthesis even more information, critical thought, and **creativity**. How does knowing all this help you? Think about the type of exams you will have to take. Do you need to simply recognize information, or should you be able to synthesize many pieces of data? If you can determine what type of exam you will have in a subject area, you can structure your note taking and study time accordingly.

As far as exams go, let me offer another piece of advice. Students are prone to ask the questions, "Will this be on the exam?" and "How much of the exam is from the book and how much from lecture?" The truth is that most professors will have a hard time answering these questions because it is almost impossible to quantify an exam. Let me instead offer you two terms that instructors use when designing examinations: *validity* and *reliability*. A test is valid if it measures what it is supposed to measure. In other words, if you read ten essays and were responsible for recognizing the author, recalling the main points, analyzing points of view, and synthesizing two of them by comparing and contrasting their main points, my test would be valid if it asked you to answer questions that allowed you to show that you mastered those tasks.

A test is reliable if students achieve consistent results. What you as a student should know is that reliability applies more to math and science courses, where each question often has one correct answer—and if two students each answer 80% of the questions correctly, their grades will be the same. Some exams cannot be judged this strictly because they are designed to let students show what they know, so two students can answer entirely differently and both be correct and get an 80% grade. This is the case with discussion questions and longer essay exams, where students offer as many different answeres as there are students. The bottom line is an ideal test will measure what students were expected to learn (often called course outcomes) and will therefore reflect the goals of the course.

Quiet, Please

Now that I have explained some essential points about teaching and learning, let's get back to managing your time in accordance with these principles. Above all, you do not want to waste your study time by doing something unproductive. Consider your answer to question 20. Can you study in a noisy environment? You need a place to study as well as time set aside for it. That place may be your room, but it need not be. If your roommate sleeps during your study time, he or she may not appreciate hearing the repetition of binomial equations. By the same token, you may not appreciate your roommate's fondness for watching television, eating, writing a letter, and playing a CD while you try to study. You can try to arrange for a new roommate, which is more difficult than it sounds, or you can approach the problem by taking actions completely under your control. If you are the quiet roommate, you can purchase some expanding foam earplugs designed for marksmen (or the wax ones that swimmers use), or noise cancelling headphones (used in music studios and by students with some disabilities). This purchase will allow you to stay in the room.

If not, this may be the start of a great adventure for you: the Quest for the Study Spot. This quest can lead you to find all sorts of wonderful places on campus. You might even wish to locate several, just in case someone else on a similar quest plants a flag on one of your spaces. Above all, have fun while exploring. Roam around campus, looking for all the quiet spots you can find. You may be perfectly happy with the library and go no further; I found my spot near the back door of the library, where I placed a chair near a window on a landing. At one college, a friend found that the coy pond worked well, except during winter or on rainy days.

You should look for places that you think people don't go (if you are a study-alone type). These can usually be found on top floors or in basements of buildings. If you're a group person, and your campus is located near quiet, all-night restaurants or coffee houses where you can meet your group for coffee and study time. Also most modern academic libraries have learning commons areas designed for group study. If you are an outdoor person, look for a bench. If you are a meticulous type of person, mark off places you have searched already on a campus map. In time, you will eventually find your study spot.

Let's digress for a moment and go back to that roommate. Suppose your big problem with your roommate occurs after you're done studying, when you're trying to get much needed rest so that you can concentrate the next day. Suppose this roommate is loud, and you cannot get any sleep. If this is the case, I suggest white noise as an alternative. You may be familiar with this concept—white noise is unfocused sound that blocks other noise. It's the kind of noise you can generate near your bed or desk with a fan, a small air purifier, or any number of gadgets designed to supply white noise. Believe me it works. I managed to write a thirty-page paper on a seventeenth-century poet with a teenager in the house—my sanity and college career were saved.

Are We Having Fun Yet?

Let's not neglect the concept of fun in time management. You should schedule fun activities just as you schedule your study time, class time, work time, and sleep time. If you know that by Wednesday the stress of the week will begin to wear on you, schedule a pick-up basketball game or card game with a group of friends, or schedule some time to game online. You also should not discount the need for spontaneous fun, like a cup of coffee and brief conversation with someone you haven't seen in a while. No matter what you do for fun, remember to limit it responsibly. If you don't, it will interfere with your coursework priorities.

Keep up with hobbies and extracurricular activities, but don't overtax yourself. I have seen too many students do this. I encountered one looking tired one day, and she confessed that she was taking nineteen credit hours, writing for the newspaper, and holding down a part time job. She was frustrated that she couldn't find time to visit her parents that weekend. I wondered that she found time to breathe.

Here, I want to give you even more helpful numbers. These will help you better understand how to manage your overall time as a college student. First off, you need to understand what it means when you hear that 12 credit hours is considered full-time (and is the base you can work from when planning your classes and financial aid). You may think you can handle more than four classes, but take my word for it—it's a good idea to begin with 12 hours only and see how well you manage. If you ace 12, you can try 15 the following semester. Keep in mind though that most students can handle 12 and not many more. Still, Americans share, among other traits, a strong work ethic, and many college students are eager to get out into the world, so many of us push ourselves beyond our capacity. The problem is that it is possible to work hard to no good end.

Remember that decision you made about succeeding in college? This means you will want to do well in all your courses, not just your favorites. You will also want to have time for those extracurricular activities that may make you more job search marketable, such as writing for the school newspaper or literary magazine, joining a student-run professional society, playing intramural sports, or being an active member of an honor society. And some students have no choice but to work, either to pay for college or feed and clothe themselves. Some first generation students even work to help their families. I, like most of your professors, understand these pressures—but you should know that you, and you alone, will have to plan how you will face them. To use a metaphor, you can choose to stick your feet in the pool, wade in waist deep, or jump into the deep end and swim or drown. Your positive attitude towards college may disappear if you put yourself in my overtaxed student's situation; you will be too exhausted to write well or study when you need to, as much as you need to. Your grades will suffer. You may even become homesick.

My advice is don't overdo it, and you will find your college experience enjoyable, perhaps even profitable. This is not to say that no individual can handle all these activities at once. Maybe you are the rare type who can. If you are, then do what is best for your long-term plans. I knew students who attended summer school and scheduled lots of hours every semester. They wanted to graduate in three years instead of four. They went on to find jobs, but sometimes they regret that they remember nothing from their classes. They cannot remember fact one about art, music, chemistry, biology, or history. And some of these people love those subject areas. Their college days whizzed by so quickly that they didn't have time (they couldn't make time) to enjoy them, and they certainly didn't have any time for friends and classes at the same time.

How to Add 48 Hours a Week Studying Time!

How you spend your weekends during your first college year is something you must factor into your time management skills. If your family was your first priority (as identifed in question 12), you may find yourself planning a trip home every weekend. This may not seem a bad idea, but it can be if you fail to take something to study with. As much as you love your family, you still will need time away from them during visits. I was under an illusion that the weekends were my free time when I began college, but I learned quickly that a student cannot succeed in college without putting some of weekend time toward study. I had to be realistic and devote at least part of Sunday to preparing for Monday's classes.

The key word in time management is balance; you will need to balance your time between your priorities and your peak times. There are also crunch times in college, and these usually fall during midterm and close to final exams. These periods of time can last weeks—and (I don't mean to scare you here, but to be realistic) can include five essays, four exams, and six class projects. How you deal with these crunch times, how you handle the enormity of these tasks, is everything.

If you paid attention to your class syllabi, you became aware of these times in the first two weeks of the semester. This allowed you to plan well ahead for crunch times. So you should have been able to plan as in this example: If I had exams in biology and art history in mid-October, a project in my psychology class due the following week, and an essay for my English class due the week after that, I would either study for the exams at least two weeks prior or finish that essay a good week before it was due. Even though class lectures may not have covered all the material, I would have read ahead and developed some idea of what I was preparing for. Once I had studied for those exams or finished that essay, I would move to the next deadline, perhaps working on that project. Above all, I would avoid confusing myself by trying to master four tasks at the same time—I may have mastered none if I had tried that much monumental multitasking. Unless you have a truly remarkable, completely organized mind, you will only end up frustrating yourself, putting off all four tasks out of fear, then doing an inferior job on everything. You would, in effect, have ensured your own failure.

Here I will return to my point, which is that you cannot succeed in college without putting some of your weekend toward study and assigments. Keep this in mind when you are filling out your calendar or planner. Look at it this way—by including weekends you give yourself two extra days every week to get your work done. I once had a cynical student who was convinced I was on a mission to destroy him personally. He wrote on one of his out-of-class assignments that he did not know how he was expected to keep a job, do his coursework in other classes, and write an essay I had assigned to him at the same time. This student was not stupid; rather he had become cynical, laboring under the impression that he could not handle the same pressures that every other student in the class faced. To make a long story short, he did badly on the essay, and may have done badly in his other courses, all because of his attitude, which was likely a product of his lack of planning. His essay displayed a lack of skill that could not be accounted for, given the three weeks he had been given to write and polish it.

Give Me A Break

Students are given various breaks during college. Most colleges and universities honor Spring Break, Summer, Fall Break, Thanksgiving, and Christmas Break. Spring Break is a great time to hit the beaches, but remember that you will be required to pick up where you left off when you return to college. It has been my experience that Spring Break invites time management problems. Travel plans change, and students do not always return the day classes resume. This is problematic because often instructors begin new topics, taking advantage of the break by arranging it so that students can start fresh when they return. In other words, you need to make strict plans so that if your classes start again on a Monday, you return Saturday and not Sunday. Even if you miss your flight or a connection you can still return in time for classes to resume.

This brings to mind another enemy of time management, which is student brooding. Students tend to brood after Spring Break, returning to their classes with a bad attitude they did not have before. Sometimes they go overboard and decide they must drop a class immediately. If such thoughts occur to you, remember this is an overreaction. If you are having difficulty in a course, you can always make an appointment for tutoring or meet with your instructor. You need to avoid thinking in terms of drastic results. Rather, you should try to find rational solutions.

Let's consider the impact decision-making ability has on time management. You will have to make many decisions during college, so start early. If you lack skill in making objective decisions, here is a handy, time-tested technique: make the old pros and cons list. Suppose you are deciding on when to schedule a biology class. Make a list of reasons to take biology now instead of later; then list all the reasons you should wait until later. Try to look at both the quantity and quality of reasons you have generated, taking into account your study style, learning style, peak times, and other variables (such as each biology instructor's reputation). This is being objective. You can get rid of trivial reasons such as not liking the professor's fashion sense or missing a favorite television program. So keep this technique in mind, especially if you said that you had trouble choosing between a number of options when faced with a problem (question 18).

Chapter Three: Stress Management

I Stress, Eustress, but We Don't Have to Be in Distress

Did you know that there are two types of stress? There is eustress, which is normal stress, perhaps even good stress, and there is distress, which is bad for you. I alluded to eustress in the previous chapter when I told the story of the student who had saved psychology as the last subject she studied each day, providing herself a pleasant experience before dinner and/or bedtime.

What you also may not know is that eustress has the power to relieve distress. If you can maximize your eustress, by creating pockets of planned stress, you can cut down your unplanned stress, or distress. Truth be told, there are many ways of coping with stress in college. My intention in this chapter is to explain several for you, in hopes of helping you find the best method for your lifestyle, strengths, and weaknesses.

Drop and Give Me Fifty

Exercise is a very effective way of coping with stress. It promotes the release of hormones that build up when we are under stress. This explains why you sometimes have more energy after exercising. Your mind may be tired, but your body is now awake, and ready for more. Keep this in mind when planning your exercise. Do not exercise too soon before going to bed, or you will have trouble falling asleep because you have ramped up your energy. Plan exercise right before you need to study for an hour or two; this way you take advantage of the energy you have gained.

Exercise is also a nice way to complement your peak times. You can actually double your peak time if you make exercise part of it. By the same token, you can use exercise to battle your body clock—if you usually go to bed early, but you find yourself needing to spend two more hours studying botany one night, you can study for 30 minutes, then exercise for 30 minutes, then study for another hour, then sleep. The exercise will not only have bought you two extra hours at a crucial time, but it will make you sleep better.

A common way to get exercise and socialize is to play sports. You don't need to qualify for the football or volleyball team; you can play intramural versions or just pick up games with friends (and strangers who will soon become friends). You should contact your Student Services office early in the semester to find out what the sports offerings are for your college. An intramural schedule may even be posted, and all you have to do is sign up to play. If perhaps you prefer more solitary sports like tennis, rowing, or endurance running, do not give up. You should have available to you various physical education courses that will allow you to participate in some organized fashion. Finally, it is very likely that your campus will have a gymnasium or fitness center (which was paid for through your student fees). This will offer you other ways to enjoy the exercise of your choice, and possibly meet some new friends.

Together or Alone

Socializing is probably the number-one way students relieve stress. Many students belong to some kind of organization, such as a fraternity or sorority, to which they can pledge early on in college. These social institutions are fine, as long as you remember that pleasant conversation and friendly gatherings occupy only one of the many squares in the table or Excel cells that lists your priorities. Review that table. Then review your situation. Do you find yourself with a group that demands too much of your time and interferes with your study plan?

If this is the case, you can either let your studies suffer, or come to the conclusion that maybe you need new relationships, with people (friends, fellow students and co-workers, possibly even significant others) who understand that your education is a priority. And although the temptation may be great, especially since alcohol gives the impression that stress has disappeared, do not, under any circumstanes, major in beer or wine consumption. Some students, particularly at large universities, get so caught up in the social whirl that they attend every party and event; they forget the reason they came to college in the first place, which was to earn a degree, get a well-rounded education, and prepare themselves for a professional life.

Binge drinking is all-to-common on many campuses. Besides being dangerous to your health and the health of others, alcohol is not going to improve your memory. Alcohol kills brain cells—it's a fact you should endeavor to remember when faced with the lure of Friday and Saturday night inebriation. The temporary feeling of well-being and stresslessness is just that—temporary. You do need to return to the real world of the classroom, exams, and projects.

Keeping in mind that you are looking for planned ways to relieve stress, you may want to schedule activities that allow you the chance to socialize. For example, you may want to schedule a date night for yourself— giving yourself one night a week or every two weeks when you concentrate on nothing but your significant other or your date. Along the same lines, you may find that a weekly movie outing with friends, especially if they are also college students, can be an excellent stress-reduction activity (albeit an expensive one, unless you meet at someone's home or dorm room to watch movies there).

The bottom line is that it is important that you enjoy your experience in college, and that college life should involve the company of other people, as well as a healthy amount of laughter, another wonderful stress reliever. You can schedule weekly or bi-weekly card and board games (these are not too old school, as any game of Cards Against Humanity will attest) or you can monitor the schedule of events posted in your campus's student union. You never know when a comedian or band will perform, or a favorite film will be shown, either on your campus or elsewhere in town. One sad fact of college life is that you have to organize all of it; you won't have a happy social life unless you do. If you are the risk-taking type, go ahead and ask that fellow student who has caught your attention to a night on the town. But don't be dissuaded if you don't have a date date. If necessary, go see a band or comedian by yourself or with a good friend. Above all, take control of your own fun. Don't wait for someone to ask you out; that time might never arrive.

And if you are the kind of person who is happy when alone, meditation is an effective way of coping with stress. You can take a course on meditation or read a book that will explain how to do it properly. What you do need to know is that you do not need to subscribe to an Eastern religion to meditate. Americans tend to think in terms of motion, always doing and accomplishing, so meditation has acquired somewhat of a mystical reputation, when in truth it is a simple practice available to people of all walks of life.

If it makes it more palatable for you, think of meditation in terms of relaxation. Start with the obvious: Lie down in a comfortable, dimly lit room or place. Beginning with your toes, think about relaxing each part of your body, moving to your feet and heels, then slowly up through the rest of your body. You should strive not to let any other thoughts enter your mind while you relax. Your mind will be clearer, and as it is with exercise, when you are finished, you will have renewed energy to face the tasks you have listed on your calendar.

Lobbying for Hobbies

Because they are the activities we enjoy most, hobbies are an effective stress-reliever. What is also great about hobbies is that there are as many as there are people. Whether you are into needlepoint, painting, drawing, carving, horseback riding, computer games, or anything else, try to give yourself some time to pursue your hobby. Just don't let your hobby take precedence over your study time.

Surfing the web and gaming online are excellent stress-relieving solitary pasttimes. You may enjoy on-line shopping, Facebook, chat apps, or you may simply like to email your friends and family. One great perk about college life is most campuses make available to their students free or low-cost internet access; some academic libraries even have laptops that can be checked out by students—and all campus libraries supply a liberal number of computers free for student use. Take advantage of this electronic media. You paid for it in your student fees.

However, remember that even though a computer, laptop, or device is a wonderful tool, they can become addictive as toys—and you didn't go to college to major in playing. The interactive nature of computers make them powerful persuaders, and some students spend many lonely hours surfing the web at the expense of their grades, money, and valuable time. If you want to maximize eustress and minimize distress, decide beforehand how much time you will spend online, then (and this is important) set an alarm so you will stop. Don't let a machine replace people and take over your social life.

Reading is another wonderful way to relieve stress. More to the point, reading is adaptable to your time management specifics. You can read magazines or newspapers quickly, so these won't use up too much valuable time. Keep in mind that you do not have to spend any of your hard-earned money by subscribing if you cannot afford to. Either your college library or your local public library will very likely subscribe to something you would like to read (although you may have to be adaptable to reading them on your laptop or device). If you have more time or are a serial reader, collections of short stories and/or novels may be to your taste. Just keep in mind you should not bring Harry Potter to class. None of your instructors wants to compete against Hogwarts for your attention. All joking aside, use pleasurable reading as a stress reliever, not a stress producer.

Routine Roulette

One of my favorite stress reducers is to break one routine. This method is very effective if you feel stuck and think you are just trudging along from day to day. Pick a routine, like how you prepare for bed—then break that routine. You can switch timing, such as instead of showering before bed, doing it in the morning, or you can simply reorganize a routine by doing the steps in a different order. It's a simple action, but even just taking a bath instead of shower can help you deal with distress. Among other things, changing a routine helps you to change your perspective.

You can do this literally. For example, if you normally sit in a chair to study, try lieing on the floor. Or if you normally relax lieing down, try standing on your head, with your legs against a wall, and observe how things look from that angle. If you are sitting in a chair, try looking at the ceiling (this stretches your neck too). You can also just visit some place on campus you have never been before. You may enjoy the view from the third floor of a new building. Believe it or not, seeing things from a different angle or position will help you feel better. Perhaps this is because of the playfulness which routine and perspective switching depends on, or perhaps it is because you simply need to not feel trapped in your surroundings (college can do that because of its demands).

Self-Improvement

Another way you can relieve stress is by improving your image. This may sound odd at first, but think of it as a change in routine, except that the routine is your sense of self. How do you accomplish this? You could try a different haircut or a total makeover. College is typically the time people start experimenting with hair color, piercings, tattoos, fashion, and lifestyle. Experimenting with defining yourself not only changes how others view you, it is an essential part of college—you are working on your identity. Sometimes you you may choose to simply change your appearance, and sometimes you may choose to work on the interior person. Maybe you want to become more honest, no longer feeling obligated to say or do things expected of you. This new honesty can be a pact both with yourself and others; this is a laudable goal that will improve your image or should relieve some of the uncontrolled stress in your life.

You may also like a classmate's tattoos. If you are comfortable with permanent changes, you may decide body art is right for you. Most people I know with tattoos spend as much time thinking about the design as getting the tattoo, to the point where the process becomes a ritual that helps them get through their days. If you'd like less permanent routine breaking, try a new hairstyle, perhaps something with a vastly different length than what you usually wear. You can purchase new clothing, learn about car maintenance, or simply look back at the list of things you would like to change about yourself in question 28. Whatever you do, remember that planned stress is always better, so decide on a course of action to accomplish these new goals to improve your image.

Give Until It Hurts

Many students volunteer with various charitable organizations in order to relieve stress, as it allows them to develop a fuller perspective (and since the last section was on reading, here I will suggest a wonderful read about gaining such perspective, Jane Stern's *Ambulance Girl: How I Saved Myself by Becoming an EMT*). My mother always told me that if I thought I had it bad, I should take a good look around. If you do the same, you will always be able to find someone who is having more trouble than you with class, and maybe that person could use a math tutor. Maybe your friend from down the hall just had a fight with her boyfriend and needs someone to listen; be that person for her. Maybe you can fix the oil leak in a classmate's car and save her the repair bill. In college, I tried to do one good thing each day for someone, whether they knew it or not. I would put change in the parking meter of the car next to mine if I saw it had expired. You get the idea: look past the end of your nose and do something for somebody else, and this will help you feel better.

You could also venture outside the confines of your college and volunteer for charitable organizations, so you might find yourself relieving stress by building houses for Habitat for Humanity. Ot you might want to feed people at a church mission. Think about the advice here; nothing makes you feel quite so good about yourself (more of that self-definition and self-improvement here) as doing something for someone else. You don't even need to belong to an organization to follow this advice.

Anxiety

I'd like to address anxiety for a moment. Many students suffer from various types of panic disorders. If you suspect that you do, seek counseling—a free service usually offered by colleges and universities. Working in your favor is the fact that newer and more effective treatments are available to help you cope with examinations and other situations that cause you to panic. Your college's Mental Health Services (possibly also called Student Health Services) will find you the right counselor, whether this person is located on campus or off. You owe it to yourself to seek treatment in order to succeed in college.

Perhaps you are familiar with another common problem facing college students, depression. We all have our moods, but clinical depression is an entirely different animal. If left untreated, sufferers may commit suicide. The remarkable thing about many people who suffer from depression is that they don't seek assistance, even though they do not enjoy being miserable. Sometimes it is because they have yet to be diagnosed; in other words, they do not know they are depressed. They may just think they are having a bad week or month, or that their energy level is down because they lack sleep. It often takes someone else's urging before such students take back control over their own lives.

I once had a student who never smiled. He was having trouble facing the challenges presented to him in college. He would make cryptic comments like, "I wonder what it's all worth anyway." He would refuse all his friends' entreaties to go out. It finally took his closest friend's intervention. This friend did not set himself up as a therapist; rather he listened. He helped his buddy work through his discomfort with psychiatrists. He even offered to accompany him to a therapist's office and simply wait outside.

Self-Assessment: Stress

Take a few moments now and make a list of the ways you like to relieve stress. Do you like to talk probblems out with friends? Do you prefer a night alone, going to a restaurant or a movie? Do you look for playful methods, such as skating to class? Ask yourself now if your method is a healthy way to relieve stress. People often resort to destructive behavior, such as binge eating or drinking, in a misguided attempt to relieve stress. Be sure that the stress relievers on your list do not boomerang. If your list looks too short, review the stress reducers I have explained in this chapter. If none of them appeal to you, an alternative is a stress management workshop on campus. Often these are offered during crunch times, midterm and final examination weeks. Take advantage of the information you learn there. Remember that there are two kinds of stress, one beneficial and one detrimental. The stress relievers I have discussed are all healthy ways to generate eustress, the kind of stess that motivates you to study for another two hours.

Chapter Four: Self-Management

Manage Thyself

Self-discipline is the cornerstone to self-management. You probably already know what motivates you—it could be the promise of chocolate, a waiting bed, the chance to sleep, or spoiling yourself with a new music CD or a live concert. Most, if not all college freshmen, are facing life on their own for the first time, finding out that things they have taken for granted, like motivation from parents (and clean laundry), can no longer be taken for granted. Combining the responsibilities of life and the demands of social life with self-motivation to meet the expectations of instructors is enough to overwhelm anyone. The only way to survive and thrive is to plan, exercise discipline, and stay healthy. In this chapter, I want to address several ways to manage your life as a student. You are now responsible for your physical and your mental health, because without these, your learning, your personal safety, and even your finances will suffer.

If You've Got Your Health....

Your well-being begins and ends with your physical health. If you are a person who catches colds easily, like me, you will need to locate the Student Health Center soon after you arrive on campus (you also may still be covered by your parents' insurance and have the option to choose a local doctor). Like in all aspects of life, it is beneficial to plan ahead, even moreso when you're ill, because it is difficult to think clearly with a sore throat, congested head, and watery eyes. Here is a helpful hint: if you have prescription medication at home (prescribed through a pharmacy near your parents and paid for by your parents), plan ahead. You'll always need to know a week in advance that you need a refill. All of these eventualities have happened to both me and my students. Those of you who have always been very healthy people have my admiration—but do know that you will likely become ill at some point during your freshman year, mainly due to an increase in responsibility (pressure) and a decrease in available sleep time.

Let's start with the basics. You must exercise in some way in order to stay healthy. There are no ifs, ands, or buts here, no reasons to the contrary—not legitimate ones anway. So, accepting this inevitability, decide early in your college career how you plan to work physical activity into your daily routine. If you want to really do yourself a favor, schedule aerobic activity at least three times each week. As a student, I tended to rely on the walking and stair-climbing opportunities made possible by a large campus;

this meant I was often able to get my exercise naturally, as part of my daily routine. I didn't have to go to a gym or recreation center. If your campus is small, take that fact into account. You'll have to find more ways to get in some excerise if none of your classes are more than 100 feet apart. It helps if you are a lover of sports and thrill at the prospect of a twice weekly basketball or softball game as part of intramurals or make-up games with friends.

If you are not into organized sports, ask yourself about your other interests. Do you like to swim or hike? Perhaps there is a bicycle trail near campus, or a rock climbing wall nearby. If you happen to be on a large campus (my graduate school campus was so large that it would take 20 minutes to walk from one end to the other), you may want to invest in a bike. Biking is not only great exercise, but it allows you to get from building to building in time to make your classes.

Most campuses have a nice quad (usually paved) which is ideal for walking, roller skating, skateboarding (if it is allowed), dribbling a basketball, or strolling. Some campuses offer large green areas, perfect for throwing a frisbee (or possibly play ultimate frisbee or frisbee golf), kicking a soccer ball, or throwing a football. Whatever your taste and skill level, take physical activity into account as you manage your time. Doing so goes a long way in maintaining your physical health.

Weighing In on Body Issues

Issues of weight gain and body image plague college students. The story of the Frehsman 15 is more than just folklore. The truth is that the changes in your lifestyle and eating habits make it very likely that your body weight will suffer, and like most freshmen, you may be horrified of the prospect of suddenly gaining 15 pounds. Obviously, you do not have to succumb to this fate. I didn't, and avoiding it was easy. All I did was eat regular meals of fairly healthy food (eating pizza three times a day may be a way to eat regular meals, but you'd better be prepared for the Freshman 50 then). I also avoided the temptation to binge and then diet—a strange diet consisting of only cans of tuna, or only bananas and saltine crackers may help you lose recently gained pounds, but you will also destroy your health.

In short, gaining the Freshman 15 is not about quantities of food; it is about neglecting a balanced diet. And if you deprive yourself of the carbohydrates needed to generate quick energy and the protein that helps build muscle, you will end up malnourished. The result will be that you'll end up doing poorly in college because of poor health. Think of it this way—you don't expect your car to run without fuel, so how can you expect your brain to function without it? Eating properly will maintain your physical health, which in turn goes a long way towards maintaining your mental health.

Body image problems are another matter. We have all seen women on television and in films who weigh 98 pounds and consider themselves obese. Obviously, these people are not viewing themselves in funhouse mirrors. Body image is psychological, based on sociological representation and societal expectations. You may not suffer from anorexia or bulimia yourself, but in college, chances are you will meet someone who is. This is one of the reasons campuses have student health centers and student services offices. You are responsible for your own mental and physical health, and it is in your own self-interest to consider yourself partially responsible for your dormmates' well-being. After all, you are now sharing a room, and everything each of you does affects the other.

Here I will reiterate a very important point I made earlier: you cannot succeed in college if you are hungry. Manage your time so that you eat three meals a day, but keep a few healthy snacks around to help you stay alert and study longer. I need not remind you the essential task of watching your blood sugar, even if you are a nondiabetic. If you ingest protein or carbohydrates, your body will digest them and convert the nutrients to energy. If you wait too long to eat, you will experience a drop in blood sugar (sugar equals energy to the muscles and organs, the brain included). This is more important than you realize; I once had a student pass out during my class. He had become so busy that he had forgotten his body needed some kind of sugar. As an undergraduate, I discovered that simply carrying around a piece of fruit with me in my backpack for just such an emergency really made a difference.

Is It Safe?

College and university administrators try very hard to keep their campuses safe, but campus security officers can do only so much. As in any city, the safety of a campus environment depends a lot on its citizens, college students like you. You should always be aware of what you need to do to address personal safety. Start with accepting that like everywhere else, crime occurs on college campuses if the conditions are right for it. But you have a good bit of control over whether you become a victim.

Protecting yourself is important, so you may want to look into a self-defense class, if your campus offers one. If not you can purchase something like pepper spray and carry it with you at all times—but keep it in your hand if you have any sense that a situation warrenting its use could present itself. In addition, it is always a good idea to travel with friends, especially after dark—you are protecting them as much as they are protecting you. If you cannot find a travel buddy after dark, check if your campus provides officers to escort students to their destinations. If you absolutely cannot find anyone to accompany you, tell a friend where you are going and when you will return. This person should be responsible enough to alert the proper authorities if you have not returned by a specific time, since time is of the essence after any crime.

People don't often think of clothing as a way to be safer, but here's a safety fashion tip: always wear light-colored clothing at night. Would-be assailants often wear dark clothing to camoflauge themselves in the dark, and if you also have dark clothing, bystanders may not see either of you if you encounter an assailant. It's a lot easier for you to disappear if people can't see you to begin with. Remember, assailants choose their victims based on the chance they can successfully commit the crime in mind.

Light-colored clothing also makes you visible to drivers, essential if you have to cross any streets or walk along any sidewalks near busy streets. If you are riding a bicycle, you should not only wear bright clothing, but also use a headlight and a rear reflector, and if you can get one, a reflective vest. You don't want to be the cause for another ghost bike.

You can do certain things that actually make you look like a potential victim. For instance, walking after dark alone, with your head down is not a good idea. Walking around intoxicated is never a good idea. Distracted people (take those earbuds out) are easy targets because they play right into the surprise element of crime. On the other hand, it is more difficult to accost someone who is striding forward quickly, listening intently for unexpected noise, eyes straight ahead or glancing around, intent on reaching a destination. Such a walker will spoil the element of surprise, minimize the window of opportunity, and give the impression he/she will fight back or flee. Finally, if you happen to be on an open carry campus and you carry a legal weapon, make sure you know how to use it safely. Too many people becomes victims of crimes committed by their own guns or hurt innocent bystanders.

Personal safety also includess safeguarding your belongings. If you are a bike rider, you should purchase a lock for your bike. If your library or other commons areas (such as the student union) offers lockers, get yourself a lock. Above all, never walk away from your belongings without asking someone to watch them. While 99 out of every 100 people is honest, it only takes that one to walk away with your bookbag (and possibly your keys), or your device or laptop (and likely all your projects and papers).

I once took a class that required a group assignment. One of the study groups left expensive textbooks on a table in the library; the students in the group wanted to take a break and walk over to the student union. When the students returned, all five of their textbooks were gone (and textbooks are in no way inexpensive, so we are talking a serious financial hit). Never simply assume other people will watch your belongings. If they aren't asked to watch your things, other students may walk away from the area, or may simply not even realize items are being stolen when someone else walks over to retrieve them. In the college library, staff can be called away to help students at any time, so never assume they can watch your items just because you are sitting in their line of vision. Unless you can afford to purchase a new laptop, don't chance leaving one behind, not even for a few minutes to go to a restroom.

Finally, if you become a victim of a crime, know what to do. Get help immediately. Emergency telephones are usually located all over campuses and do not need to be dialed—if you pick up the receiver, the distress call is automatically transferred to campus security. If you cannot find an emergency phone, call campus security or 911. After you've been victimized, do not wash yourself in any way. Don't even dust yourself off. You do not want to destroy evidence and hamper an investigation that will lock up the criminal and make your campus safer for future students.

If safe and possible, do not stray far from the crime scene. Your mind was moving very quickly when the attack occurred, and you may not even be able to recognize the exact location after several minutes. If you have a piece of paper or a device or laptop, begin writing a physical description of your assailant, including eye color, height, weight, clothing, hair color, unusual identifying marks, scars, or anything that can be used to identify the criminal. You will forget details as time goes on and your mind does what it naturally does: attempt to block the traumatic incident from your memory. Take advantage of short-term memory and get that description written. I realize that this is an unpleasant subject, but do keep this advice in mind if you are victimized. Your actions will save the next potential victim, possibly even a friend of yours. You can do nothing to change what happened, but you can do a lot to make sure no one else gets hurt.

Managing Your Daily Routines

Managing yourself also includes many mundane, daily and weekly tasks like doing laundry. Nobody wants to be the roommate who piles clothes on the floor and has to pick up underwear and smell it to see if it's clean, so it will benfit you to learn about daily laundry upkeep. First off, make sure you have some place to put your clothes as you wear them and get them dirty. You will want to learn how to sort your clothing based on the need to machine launder, hand wash, and dry clean pieces. If you take clothes to your parents on a weekly or bi-weekly visit, you will not have to find a laundromat, but if you do, work laundry day into your study time schema. There is no reason you should have to sit there and stare at washing machines and dryers, when you can be reading assignments in preparation for courses or studying for exams while your laundry is being done.

And speaking of studying, you will want to study on life skills associated with laundering clothing, such as when and how to use bleach, how to correctly use laundry detergent, what cycle to set machines on so as not to ruin your clothing, and when to add detergent and softener to water (these will likely be skills you were never taught at home—fortunately youtube offers many helpful skills videos). You will also need to learn to correctly fold and hang clothes so that they do not wrinkle or tear—part of feeling better about yourself and building a positive attitude is being able to dress well when needed, so clothing upkeep is important (here is a helpful hint: you can hang or fold jeans and slacks, but you must match up the leg seams perfectly first, or they will get wrinkled and hang strangely on your body). In fact, clothing upkeep is essential. If you do it daily for a few minutes, you ultimately save time and reduce stress, both of which are beneficial to you at crunch times.

You'll also want to spend a few minutes each day making sure that you properly care for delicate clothing, so that when you need to do that group presentation or elevator pitch, you will look the part (which can be part of your grade). You'll want to learn how to deal with clothes that need to be dried flat on a towel or hung over a shower rod, properly buttoned. You'll want to learn how to iron clothing, or how to avoid having to iron it if possible. You likely won't have an ironing board, so you'll need to learn optional methods, such as a towel placed on the floor.

In addition to managing your laundry, you will need to manage your daily room upkeep. It is difficult to study in a room piled high with books, so decide when to clean and organize. Despite the fact that a popular (but helpful) way to put off studying is a cleaning marathon, you should clean daily, at least one area of a dorm room, or one room of an apartment, each day.

Do not fall into the trap of thinking that you can eat and not clean afterwards. Unless you know a Hogwart's magic spell, clean dishes just won't happen. You will need to keep dishes clean to avoid the spread of disease and keep insects (especially roaches and flies) away. It does no good to leave dirty dishes lieing around, even for just one night. Wash them at least once a day. You do not need dish detergent if it is unavailable, but you do need extrememly hot water to kill germs and bacteria. If you use any kind of soap, rinse dishes thoroughly, then dry them, as some soap residues can make you ill.

Our Bodies, Ourselves

No one ever wants to talk about it, but personal hygiene is an essential part of the freshman experience. You should always maintain personal standards in this area. No matter how busy you get, bathe or shower each day, and wash your face at least once in the morning and once at night. Above all, take good care of your teeth; dental visits are expensive and painful, so always brush and floss daily.

Become a smart consumer of personal care products (college may be the first time you have personally shopped for these items). Read labels for ingredients, and use the Internet to learn about what these ingredients are (even if you're not a chemistry major, you should know about any chemicals you put into or on your body). Refresh your memory on preventative measures for common ailments like athlete's foot and skin rashes. Finally, use your library to keep up with recent studies, such as a recent one which found that you can shorten the duration of a cold with zinc tablets or a few drops of echinacea in coffee or tea. You may not enjoy the way they taste, but you will feel better sooner than if you had treated your cold with over-the-counter remedies like antihistamines.

Also remember that an ounce of prevention is worth more than a pound of cure. No matter where your campus is located, flu season will hit, and bouts of influenza will make their journey around campus. You college's health center will very likely offer immunization, and you can stock up on vitamin C and the aforementioned echinacea, among other herbs and vitamins. You don't want to get sick, because the only effective way to treat a flu is rest and fluids, and the last thing you need is to be bedridden with fever instead of in class.

If you do fall ill, take on the responsibility of keeping up with your coursework. You should always contact your instructors as soon as possible to explain the problem and find out how you can get any notes you missed. Remember, you can study in bed, and if you feel up to it, keep up with your class work. Professors know that students become ill, but they also know that illness is an excuse to miss class, not a legitimate reason to miss deadlines or do poorly on assignments; they too have been to college, and they have worked through illnesses—and they know the difference between circumstances beyond one's control and poor time management and planning skills.

But more than that, they know how difficult it is for students, so they are usually amenable to extensions on deadlines—if you are responsible enough to contact them early on with a legitimate reason like illness. Just be wary of going to the well too often. I have had more than one student who asked for an extension, then took advantage of my patience by continually asking for even more time, even one who had a legitimate reason—he was ill at midterm (and had also asked to be given a make-up exam, which I granted). All of you instructors will have policies for late assignments; learn them and keep them in mind, should you suffer a health emergency.

Be Mindful of Your Frame of Mind

Many college students face personal crises at various times during their four years as undergraduates. Some have relatives who are in poor health, or grandparents who are elderly and need special care. These family issues can weigh a student down. Grief is difficult for everyone, but in college, as in the work world, you will be expected to recover quickly from family problems and resume your responsibilities. When such problems occur, let your emotions surface so you can deal with them, but try as hard as you can to stick with your schedule. Depending on the severity of the family problem, you may need some time off. If this occurs, take a week, and if you still find your responsibilities too difficult to bear, talk to your professors and your advisor. You may be eligible to take an I grade—an incomplete—as long as it doesn't take you too long to get the work done (most incompletes must be rectified by the end of the following semester). You may even consider taking a semester off, rather than failing your classes as a result of your grief. It all depends on how you deal with distress.

I am the type of person who feels better when she is busy. Keeping busy helped me to survive 13 years of uninterrupted education during a span of time when my grandmother, uncle, great uncle, father, and brother died. You may be different, but if you do decide to take a break for the sake of your overall education, ask yourself what you would do during the time off. Would you join a grief support group? Everyone handles grief differently, and just as I assured you earlier that you can plan your personal time, your classes, and your social life to achieve stress management, I assure you that you can manage your grief—as long as you find an effective method that works for you.

Above all, give yourself time to think about the issue which has caused your grief. If you are dealing with a loss, use your memories to help you cope: look at photos, listen to music, or talk to a shared friend who also suffered the loss. If possible, keep a journal to record thoughts and activities. And don't be ashamed to cry, as much as you like. Walking around with bottled-up emotions is an unhealthy approach. Grief is a loss, and loss is a powerful feeling.

This may sound a bit odd when you first read it, but you can develop a grief plan. This is particularly helpful if you take your grief very personally and become very angry. If you find yourself ruminating on the reason the grief occurred, and you never get past that stage, you will adversely affect your student life—and I assure you that no one has ever died with the express purpose of costing someone an education. You simply cannot personalize adverse events which you did not cause. What you can do is soul-search.

For example, if you lose a loved one and find yourself stuck at anger, ask yourself why you're angry. Perhaps you will be missing the emotional support you got in the past, or perhaps the loss has left you with a empty spot. What you can do is develop a plan—it can involve a good friend, an activity, or a group that will provide emotional support you so desperately need. Your plan can be to plunge right back into your routine. I was actually comforted by the fact that I was responsible for teaching four classes the semester my brother died. The new responsibilities were a godsend—they made me feel needed and valued. I did feel rushed and slightly resentful right after his funeral, but I soon began to look past the end of my nose and concentrate on others, in this case students and colleagues who needed me.

Plunging back into a routine to help you work through grief can help you recover in a healthy way. Dealing with grief has to be part of time management. You can even go as far as to set aside a fixed time to grieve. Do not spend too much time doing this, or you will feel worse (but again, give grief its time). My mother had a healthy attitude toward grief that you may find encouraging: she thought of death as a beginning. You do not need to be a religious person to find satisfaction in this idea. If you lose someone you admire, that loss can mark a new beginning in your life, a time when you resolve to change yourself for the better.

Ending relationships will also cause grief, especially for non-traditional students who are divorcing, especially if they are parents. For the younger student, a relationship change can occur when his/her parents decide to divorce, after having satisfied in large part their responsibilities toward their children. By the same token, your parents may turn you loose, emotionally and financially once you go off to college. Again, you cannot personalize grief (in this case homesickness). I can assure you that hardly any parents do any of these things to cut themselves off from their children.

Also, you will discover that not only the circumstance, but its repucussions, are beyond your control. If you watch your parents divorce, you may develop the feeling of being torn between your parents, pressured to take sides—knowing that any side you take is the wrong side. You are in a double bind as a college student: you have begun to relate to your parents as an adult, not a child, but you feel like you are still their child. Now that they see you as an adult, they may share their emotions with you more openly than they did when you lived at home. My best advice is that you listen without attempting to fix the problem. You will feel caught in the middle, and you may want to seek some counseling. You might also adapt the strategies I explained earlier about managing grief, because divorce is a loss of the image you always had of your parents as one unit and not as two separate individuals with different lives.

Self-Medication

Every human being needs to avoid destructive behavior. For the student, this means not attempting to deal with stress in unhealthy ways, such as dependence on illegal drugs, misused prescriptions, or alcohol. Unless you grew up in a rough neighborhood or a truly dysfunctional home, the chances are you will encounter more drug and alcohol use in college students than you have ever seen before. In fact, drugs and alcohol may be part of the social life to which some of your newly made friends subscribe. I can tell you that both are addictive for a very good reason—while chemically altered, your mind and body become more relaxed or energized (depending on what effect you are aiming for and what chemical you use). However, you have a really good reason to avoid imbibing—you simply cannot learn if your mind is clouded by chemicals.

Overview

Self-management takes discipline. Often the only person you have to rely on as a college student is yourself. You are responsible for your mental and physical health, your personal safety, and your daily routine, all the while avoiding destructive behavior—even if faced with a personal crisis like the death of a loved one or a divorce in your family. You are also responsible for your sexual health.

This area of your life is part of personal responsibility. For some reason beyond my grasp, college students too often fail to plan ahead regarding sex. They forget to take responsibility for their actions, and are honestly surprised at their consequences. If you are going to succeed in college, you will need to be responsible for your sexual health. If you lack information, do some research. Do not rely on secondhand information that you have no way of verifying. Look at scientific studies with reliable statistics, and read medical journals and reputable websites (here your librarian can help).

Chapter Five: Relationships

Manage a Relationship? Surely You Jest

No matter how young you are, you probably know by now that the words *manage* and *relationship* seem at odds. Relationships may seem more like uncontrollable creatures that grow at their own rate than they seem part of a manageable life. Sometimes, relationships can be so unpredictable that it seems a mystery why they succeed or fail. However, you will discover in college, as in later life, that managing relationships is essential in keeping you happy, and happiness goes a long way towards making you successful in college. Truth be told, just like your body, your stress, and your classes, you can manage your relationships. They do require time and effort—but they can succeed, whether you are coming into them as a complete novice (many by college have not yet had a long-term relationship) or an old pro (if you are a non-traditional student with years of marriage under your belt).

Communication is the cornerstone of any good relationship. You and your significant other may be as different as the sun and the moon, but often you can work out important differences if you communicate effectively. For starters, doomed communication between two people often features phrases like "you always" or "you never." Such blanket statements may help you express anger or frustration, but they do little to open a line of communication; they make the other person defensive and open up the door for quibbling (nit-picking details instead of dealing with the issue, as in for example, a retort like "well just last month I ..."). Granted, it will be difficult for you, as it would be for me or anyone else, to unlearn bad communication skills, but what I hope to do here is offer alternatives and helpful hints.

Change the Perspective

Rather than use language that attacks the other person (let's face it, the minute you say the word *you* in an argument, it's clear you're in attack mode), try changing the language to being about expression. In other words, you can simply change the subject of a sentence to first person, *I*. So instead of saying "you always pick the movie," say "I would like to pick the movie this time." Instead of declaring the blanket statement "you never take me out to eat," try expressing what you really mean: "I really would love it if you would take me to dinner tonight." This is a very simple technique that lets the other person know how you feel or what you want, without making it sound as though you are judging or criticizing.

Now don't get me wrong. I am not saying that you should never criticize someone you care about. After all, I've been married, and I know better (wink wink). But when I did have to criticize, I always remembered that a critic is someone who objectively reviews in order to offer suggestions for improvment; I also remembered that the reason I was critical in the first place was part selfish—I wanted to make my husband into a better marriage partner for me—and part selfless—I wanted to make his life better because I care about him.

Change the Tone

Think about movie reviews you have read. They are based on certain objective criteria, like whether the plot makes sense, the dialogue sounds true to life, the cinematography engages viewers, and the acting is believable. The critic proceeds in an organized fashion to analyze each of these criteria. She may like the plot but find the dialogue choppy. She may love the acting of the lead, but be disappointed in the supporting actors. By placing all these aspects of the overall item for review into perspective, she will be able to give a more objective review. There is a big difference between objectivity (sometimes called the logical approach), and subjectivity (sometimes called the emotional approach).

So how does this apply to relationships? Suppose you want to legitimately criticize a person, and be objective. A statement like "the way you fold towels is wrong" is subjective—there are many ways to correctly do this task, and methods are a matter of taste. On the other hand, a statement like "if you fold the towels this way, they will fit better on the shelves" is logical and more objective. Obviously, there is probably one way to fold towels where they will fit the shape of a shelf better. You can take it one step further and make the criticism constructive by saying "let me show you a way to fold them that will make them fit better on the shelf." This makes your criticism come across as both positive and objective, plus it explains the reason the difference in methods matters, something most reasonable people will respect.

Another important aspect of communication is being able to safely express our feelings to one another. It is comforting to talk to your partner after a difficult day and explain how exhausted and frustrated you feel about your day. A good friend will be ready to listen to your problems, but no one likes to be constantly around a Sad Sack or Debbie Downer. If you find yourself constantly unloading your feelings like a dump truck backing up to a landfill every day, you will wear out your friends and your partner. This is the reason it's important to share good news whenever possible and to sometimes just be upbeat. Communication works in two directions. If you feel that it is everyone else' responsibility to listen to your complaining on a daily basis, no one will value spending time with you. Communication is about being reasonable and fair. To be reasonable you will need to think about the right time for complaints and anxiety; to be fair you will need to offer your ear in turn. Happiness is about balance.

Comfortable Conversations

Communication should allow us to feel vulnerable, with both our friends, relatives, and partners. In a good relationship, I should feel comfortable talking about everything, including my fears (for example, that I am frightened of failure, too much pressure, and snakes). I need to be confident that my fears won't be laughed at, and that I won't be told that I am being silly. I should feel confident that I won't be called names.

If you are unable to feel vulnerable in your conversations, this is a sign that you should be re-evaluating that relationship. This, too, is a two-way process. Your friends, family, and partners should feel the same comfort. Your boyfriend may be heavily muscled and proud of his masculinity, but deadly afraid of speaking in public, and you should be able to listen and sympathize if he needs to talk about it. Good communication is what allows relationships to last through difficult times.

Unfortunately, long-distance relationships are common among college students—and these present serious challenges in communication, as it becomes even more important because you will need to have people to talk to when you are under the pressure of an academic life. You can write letters and email, video chat, and phone chat with family, friends, and other loved ones, but these communication mediums all have limitations. Even if you are able to plan regular trips to see people you miss, you will no doubt notice that such relationships are difficult to maintain. You'll need to set up rules for any long-distance relationship. For example, you'll need to determine how often you can find time to talk to the people from whom you are separated. Not only will you have a tight schedule, but they will have schedules of their own. You may even need to plan what days and times you can call people you miss, so time management and planning will become even more important than if you lived close to these people.

Hearing Our Parent's Voices

There are all sorts of forces at work in our minds that we may not even know about. By now I am sure you have heard the psychological theory that we all look for a partner who reminds us of our mother or father. Most college-aged students try very hard to avoid doing this, but the truth is that even if you find someone you believe is nothing like your opposite sex parent, someday you will encounter a conflict with that person that repeats an issue that you associate with your childhood and your parents. This is independent of personality traits.

For example, your partner may be a tight-wad, someone who can never bring himself to spend as much money as you would like for a Saturday dinner night. This annoys you, and you take it as a sign that your partner is insensitive to your feelings. Suddenly, you realize that, without being conscious of it, somewhere in the back of your mind you are reacting the way you have seen a parent act.

This is not to get into a complicated discussion on genetics or psychology; suffice it to say that you are not a carbon copy of either your father or your mother. You are a unique individual, albeit one who is a product of your parents' DNA, experiences, and beliefs. Environment does have its effect on you, and that is where this repetition of the past comes in. By now you may be asking why this digression into childhood is important in a discussion about communication and college life. Not to keep you in further suspense, I will get to the point: you need to be aware that the communication you have with friends, partners, and professors may not even be about the issue at hand; you may simply be unconsciously dealing with your parents and your conflicts with them.

This is important to understand, because once you leave home, your professors become your new authority figures, in a way that your high school teachers never were because when you were in high school, you still had your parents as your authority figures. If you leave home for college, you will be looking to project your beliefs about authority onto someone else, most likely your professors. Now stop and think about how you reacted to your parents' authority. You should be aware that you may reproduce this behavior onto your professors, even though they had nothing to do with your upbringing.

Truth be told, you will need to resolve conflicts and power struggles in all your relationships. Roommate conflicts can be as small as arguments over who cleans a dirty floor. Partner conflicts can be as large as who handles finances. The secret to all these power struggles is effective, always honest communication, communication that never resorts to name-calling or threats of violence. Through honest communication, you can work on the art of compromise—this allows both you and the person with whom you are compromising with to get some part of the desired outcome. This can include sharing responsibility equally (such as alternating who cleans a dirty floor or who gets the credit cards).

This may require some loosening up of traditional gender roles. If you come to the table of communication with a strictly traditional understanding of gender roles, and across from you is the most liberal person you have met to date, expect issues with both the type and number of power struggles. At some point, someone in a power struggle needs to give up something, or a truce will not be achieved. In the case of roommates or partners, this could manifest itself in cleaning chores. With professors, this can manifest itself when a male student cannot bring himself to respect a female professor, or when a male professor unconsciously always calls on male students in class. The ugly truth is that some academic fields are still male-dominated, so if you encounter what seems like sexist behavior, try honest, objective communication.

For example, if you are on a group project and see that you are being ignored because you are the only female in a group of males (or vice-versa), point to facts such as your performance on assignments to make the point that you are being underestimated and undervalued. If you find yourself at fault for not recognizing a fellow student's work because of his/her sex, apologize—apologies can smoothe over problems when they are appropriate and sincere. If you are the victim of sexism, do not take it lightly, and do not just sit quietly back and keep a list of grievances in your head. This will cause a build up of anger and frustration. Deal with relationship issues as they occur, one at a time, when the issues are small and easy to identify. Otherwise, you are headed for a marathon argument over vague impressions—these are always counterproductive.

Knowing a Bad Relationship

A good relationship will involve the best aspects of positive communication: trust, vulnerability, optimism, and adaptability. You will know bad relationships because they will lack these elements. Destructive relationships are those that go one step beyond and become abusive, emotionally and/or physically. As a young adult, you will need to learn to protect yourself. The first step is realizing that you never have to accept a relationship with someone who calls you names, constantly criticizes you, or humiliates you. Your self-confidence will slowly erode if you stay in this relationship, and that will bleed over into your performance as a student, not to mention that such abuse will add stress to your life.

All human beings who are respectful themselves should expect to be treated with respect. You shouldn't even have to think twice about what to do if you become a victim of physical abuse; it is simply something you should never put up with. There are psychological reasons people allow abuse in their relationships, not the least of which being that it can be a carry over from the family unit (if that unit was abusive). In short, people who have been abused in the past are more likely than those who were not to become involved in abusive relationships. The bottom line, however, is that no one thrives when abused.

When I was attending college, I worked with a young woman who had been abused as a child. She also had to witness her parents' abuse of one another. She once explained to me that her father used to beat up her mother, until she shot him; she added that after that incident, they "got along." She added, "like married people should." Her statement revealed an ugly truth that helped me to understand why she was currently in her own abusive relationship—she had come to accept that what she witnessed was the norm, not the exception. She had nothing to compare her parents' relationship to.

Later, when I asked her about bruises on her arm, she said that her husband had caused them because she didn't clean the house that day. Sadly, and tellingly, she added "I guess I deserved it." I remained her friend despite the fact that I strongly disagreed with her logic. What she should have done was escape the abusive relationship and prosecute her abuser, rather than allow him to be a Jekyll and Hyde person. A good relationship is not one where you are always waiting for an abusive person to be in a good mood— this is advice you should use when forming your friendships, love relationships, and later your professional relationships (bosses can be abusive as well).

It is unlikely you will encounter an abusive instructor or professor, as usually they are not retained at universities and colleges, but if you do, you should talk to your campus's student services people to find out your rights. The solution may be as simple as dropping the abusive professor's class and taking the subject matter with someone else, or it may be as complicated as filing an official grievance. Whatever your campus's policies, you need to familiarize yourself with them and then you need to be vocal about getting your questions answered—colleges are not staffed with mind readers, but they are staffed with helpful professionals who know what to do in any situation, including abuse.

Old Friends and BFICs

In college you will make new friends, and your relationships with them will be important. Like love relationships, friendship is about trust and vulnerability. Same-sex friendships usually have other dimensions as well. Women often feel more comfortable discussing their private lives with other women; some see this as a better option than talking to their partners directly. Good friends can help us sort out our problems and solve our conflicts. Our friends listen to us when we complain, and they offer sympathy.

You may prefer brutally honest friends, the type who will tell you if a hair style or fashion choice is a mistake, or you may prefer those who will compliment you no matter what. Whatever your preference, ask yourself if your friendships are satisfying to you. A friend should make you feel better after you talk to him or her, with the main exception being times that are rough or trying for both or either of you. If you find a friend to be a negative influence, or you feel as though you have been run over by a bus after talking with him or her, you may need to re-assess your friendship.

This does not mean that as you mature you will outgrow all your friends. To this day, I have friends I went to high school with, but I did cut ties with those who were causing me stress while I was trying to become a successful college student. However, I made new friends at each college campus where I got my degrees. You should as well, if you take the time and make the effort. And there is a good reason you'll need to make these new friends in college—you are going to discover that your old friends will not understand your need for exacting time management and planning. Even those who went on to find full time jobs won't quite appreciate what it means to have to take work home *every single night*, or why it is so important that you spend six hours studying for an exam. Most of them will not understand why, when they call you to come over for movie night, you need to say no. Even if you are the world's biggest football fan, you may have to turn down the invitation to watch Monday Night Football (possibly for the first time ever).

The truth is that it takes a college student to understand the stresses of college on a student, so you will want to make some friends among your classmates, no matter what level of education you are pursuing. College gets progressively harder, so freshmen will not get the stresses that are faced by seniors, and seniors have no idea what master's students go through, and master's students have it easy compared to PhD students.

So your task will be to meet and befriend people who are, for want of a better metaphor, in the same boat as you. There are easy ways to do this, and all of them involve your getting over any shyness you may have. You can simply invite someone from class to study with you; this works especially well if you are strong in the study area, which gives your friendship added value, from your friend's point of view. You will also be surprised at how readily the smartest student in class will agree to a study partner—he or she may also be in real need of a collegial friendship and will jump at the chance to form one. On the other hand, you may find people who aren't great study partners, but are wonderful friends for down times, especially if you share interests.

It is never a bad idea to invite a new friend to see the latest blockbuster movie (or indie flick, if your tastes dictate). Like you, these potential friends are probably missing the people they normally see films with. You can also find fellow students who are tired of cafeteria food and would like to try some of the nearby restaurants (or pubs, if you are of legal drinking age). This not only allows you to make a new friend, but also learn about your college town. The upside of making these new friends is that you may keep some far beyond your college years. I have made friends who went on to become accountants, insurance agents, professors, and lawyers; the fact that we did not pursue the same career paths did not destroy our friendships.

For All You Non-Traditionals (If You Have Children)

Not all college freshmen are straight out of high school, and this section is for those of you who have already gone out into the world and started a family. If you have children and you are in college, you have special concerns which will determine how well you succeed. More than any other type of college student, a non-traitional who happens to be a parent has to be able to manage time. Think of it this way: managing your time is part of managing your relationship with your children. The important thing to remember is that you are not attempting the impossible—you can do it.

Start by reviewing the time management strategies I discussed earlier. You will *really* need them. If you paid careful attention to those strategies, you probably noticed that the most important aspect to time management is planning, or scheduling. This may sound counter-intuitive, but you should schedule time with your children, and do it strategically. For example, if your children have homework, plan your own schedule so that you work on assignments or study with them, preferable in a shared space such as the kitchen table, or in a den or library. Learning to co-habit an environment with others while doing your own work (and often not interacting) is absolutely essential if you are going to have an academic or professional career, so start perfecting that skill now. I have a friend who has an PhD and is in a relationship with someone who also has a doctorate. The two write books together and even teach together, but most of the time they spend together is either in two separate rooms writing on two computers, or at a table in a coffee shop together, working on two computers (they also make sure to find time to go off somewhere and have fries or dinner together with no work, or to watch a couple of episodes of a favorite television series on Hulu, Britbox, or Netflix).

If you require absolute silence, schedule your study time after you put your children to bed. This is where planning and discipline are important—you cannot afford to waste time if time is precious, so avoid television and other distractions after your children are asleep. The key here for everyone involved is discipline. Children must understand that they will need to observe a particular, consistent bed time, or that when they work in the same room with you that all involved will work, and not chat, listen to loud music, sing, or text (or use other social media). You, of course, will have to be similarly disciplined and consistent. I have a friend who earned her degree this way, so I know it works.

Your life is full now with work, school, and children, so I would also suggest that you schedule the children's time so that they help around the house. Whether you give them an allowance or simply make chores a part of their daily existence, make a schedule of tasks. These tasks should be time and outcome specific, and should be catered to each child. Very young children can dust low tables if there are no breakable items involved. Older children can wash and fold laundry and can wash and/or dry dishes. More responsible children can cook. This will make more time for you—or you can schedule your time so that task time is also parent-child time. This allows you to show your love for your children through time spent and stick to your list of priorities (in order to succeed in both your relationships and in college). Good relationships, even with your own family, do not spring up out of the ground and grow magically; like anything else that you value in your life, relationships take time, effort, and perspective.

Postscript: Final Thought

I wish you an enjoyable, productive college experience. College can be the best time of your life, even though it can be the most stressful. My hope is that with some of the suggestions and hints that you have found throughout this text, you will be able to maximize enjoyment and minimize frustration. Further, I hope that some of the methods that you take from this text, or those that you create yourself based in information you read here, will prove useful not just in the four years you spend as an undergraduate, but also for the years afterwards, whether you decide to get a master's degree (and dare I say a PhD?) or go out into the work world to begin your life as a contributing member of society. In fact, my sincere hope is that some of these skills will find their way into your family life—and will be passed down for generations so that your children and grandchildren will know how to plan their time in such a way as to maximize their success and happiness.

About Nighthawks

Nighthawks Publishing is an independent publisher of academic texts. Our intent is to offer opportunities for scholars in student success, education, art, film studies, literature, information science, and musicology to have a voice in the academic print world. Headquartered in Northampton, Massachusetts, home of Smith College and center of The Five Colleges Area, it is run by two academics with more than ten books and three dozen articles between them.

About This Book

The Nighthawks team that worked on this text are two scholars with PhDs in English-Literature. With decades of teaching and administrative service behind them, they have more than done their time in academia.

Like its sibling publishing imprint of MLMC Media, Gothic and Main, Nighthawks strives to give independent authors a voice and more control over their manuscripts. This text is our response to colleagues who find it increasingly difficult to publish in academic fields because their ideas go against the rigid mindsets and stylistics of their disciplines. *The Nighthawks Guide to Succeeding in College* does not fit a preconceived model because we are not a publisher that thinks of itself as a company, creating books primarily as commodities. Our aim is to create a guide that contains practical, helpful information on succeeding in college, not a loosely connected narrative of buzzwords and clichés.

As its name suggests, Nighthawks is run by hard-working night owls whose goal is to produce groundbreaking academic texts. Its Editors in Chief have lived entire lives in the college environment, so they have a great interest in helping students succeed. The text's primary author, a retired college instructor with a PhD in English, wrote this guide for her niece, who did succeed in college, earning her own degree with the manuscript under her arm.

www.ingramcontent.com/pod-product-compliance
Lightning Source LLC
Chambersburg PA
CBHW032028040426
42448CB00006B/762